ALWAYS WAS ALWAYS WILL BE

THE CAMPAIGN FOR JUSTICE AND RECOGNITION CONTINUES

THOMAS MAYO

Hardie Grant

EXPLORE

Published in 2024 by Hardie Grant Explore, an imprint of Hardie Grant Publishing

Hardie Grant Explore (Melbourne)
Wurundjeri Country
Building 1, 658 Church Street
Richmond, Victoria 3121

Hardie Grant Explore (Sydney)
Gadigal Country
Level 7, 45 Jones Street
Ultimo, NSW 2007

www.hardiegrant.com/au/explore

A catalogue record for this book is available from the National Library of Australia

Hardie Grant acknowledges the Traditional Owners of the Country on which we work, the Wurundjeri People of the Kulin Nation and the Gadigal People of the Eora Nation, and recognises their continuing connection to the land, waters and culture. We pay our respects to their Elders past and present.

For all relevant publications, Hardie Grant Explore commissions a First Nations consultant to review relevant content and provide feedback to ensure suitable language and information is included in the final book. Hardie Grant Explore also includes traditional place names and acknowledges Traditional Owners, where possible, in both the text and mapping for their publications.

Cover design note:
Australian Aboriginal Flag designed by Mr Harold Thomas
Torres Strait Islander Flag designed by Mr Bernard Namok

Always Was, Always Will Be
ISBN 9781741179279

10 9 8 7 6 5 4 3 2 1

Publisher
Roxy Ryan and Danielle Dominguez
Project editors
Bernadette Foley and Amanda Louey
Editor
Bernadette Foley
Editorial assistance
Rosanna Dutson
Proofreader
Puddingburn Publishing
First Nations consultant
Jamil Tye, Yorta Yorta
Cover design
Jenna Lee, Gulumerridjin (Larrakia), Wardaman and KarraJarri
Cartoon
Cathy Wilcox
Typesetting
Mike Kuszla
Production manager
Simone Wall

Colour reproduction by Splitting Image Colour Studio

Printed and bound in Australia by IVE.

The paper in this book is FSC® certified. FSC® promotes environmentally responsible, socially beneficial and economically viable management of the world's forests.

FSC
www.fsc.org
MIX
Paper | Supporting responsible forestry
FSC® C018183

I dedicate this book to the Elders and ancestors who had hope for a better future, despite the feet of the British colonisers on their throats. They then endured the ignorance and disregard toward them from a young nation, and yet they succeeded.

Also, to the young leaders coming through today, who will hone their rage into a key that opens hearts and minds, rather than a blade that will sever support.

And finally, to the hearts and minds that are open.

Aboriginal and Torres Strait Islander peoples are advised that this publication contains the names of deceased people.

Forewords

Emeritus Professor John Maynard
Worimi man from the Port Stephens region of NSW

Always was, always will be – powerful Aboriginal words of political resistance that have echoed and resonated across the decades of struggle.

Thomas Mayo's book is much more than an overview of ongoing campaign for the Uluru Statement from the Heart, the subsequent referendum on a Voice to Parliament and its heartfelt loss. It is a very personal reflection of the inner workings and make-up of the man Thomas Mayo. The reader is taken on a fishing expedition with Thomas and his family in the aftermath of the referendum to begin his own healing process. It reveals a proud Indigenous man and loving family man. It looks back to his years growing up and the many influences that have shaped his thinking. It shows the inspiration and joy he has in belonging to the Maritime Union of Australia and the strength he has gained from the wharf environment. On the wharf he continues the long tradition of many famous Aboriginal dockworkers and political warriors, including my grandfather Fred Maynard, Jack Hassen, Bill Onus, Reg Saunders, Joe McGuinness, 'The Fox' Chicka Dixon, and Terry O'Shane, to name but a few.

Thomas, like many Aboriginal people, carries deep disappointment in the referendum result, but as this book demonstrates, he remains focused with hope in the future. There is no bitterness carried in

Thomas over the result or the shocking personal attacks against him in the media throughout the campaign. He was demonised and constructed to be a radical ratbag who hated the country. Anyone who knows the real Thomas Mayo can testify that this is far from the truth of this man. Across the last 230-odd years we as Indigenous people have suffered many setbacks and disappointments, but we pick ourselves up, walk and fight on.

The book does not just examine the rollercoaster ride of excitement and disappointment connected with the referendum but examines the long Aboriginal and Torres Strait Islander culture and history of the continent and political struggles across the last century.

Thomas remains focused on a time when all peoples of this continent can join hands and walk together to a future that is just and equitable for all Australians of all backgrounds. The sad reality of the referendum was that Indigenous people of the country were willing to embrace with all to share the country's richest treasure, and that is upwards of 65,000 years of cultural and spiritual connection to the continent. It was simply the greatest opportunity to heal from the past and move forward together. Thomas offers advice on where to go next from here to achieve genuine improvements to Indigenous lives and outcomes in the country.

In conclusion, I congratulate Thomas on a great book and express my admiration for his strength, dignity and courage across the years he stood for the Uluru Statement and the Voice. In the final analysis this book provides genuine hope and hope is the message.

Armani Francois
Eastern Arrernte and Torres Strait Islander woman

My name is Armani Francois, I am nineteen years old, and I am a Central Eastern Arrernte, Torres Strait Islander and Mauritian woman with a bloodline rich in advocacy and leadership.

From my first breath, I have been inspired and enthused by my Elders, ancestors, and culture. They have guided me to what I do today.

I work as an Indigenous youth support worker in Alice Springs, which has always been Mparntwe to the First Peoples. My role is to help the most disadvantaged people in our country – the youth in the Northern Territory. I also sit on the NT Round Table as a representative from Alice Springs, I was a youth delegate at the Hands on Heart National Youth Conference, and I am currently a member and mentor for Youth Parliament NT.

On my Country, you cannot miss the inequalities we face as Aboriginal and Torres Strait Islander people. The poverty and social problems are heartbreaking. But I wonder if Australians are as heartbroken as I am.

The Aboriginal youth in Mparntwe, and in other towns around the country, are always in the national headlines. They have been labelled as raging savages. Appallingly, on social media and boldly on the streets, people have been death wishing our kids and characterising them as people they are not.

Why can't people see that kids are not the problem?

What does it take for Australia to wake up to the fact that our children are born into cycles of poverty?

The kids that I support are trapped in the wrongs that have happened for generations. They will be trapped until there are permanent frameworks that are culturally, mentally and physically safe for them.

At work – and I don't see it as a job, I see it as a responsibility – I have equipped myself with the armour of knowledge. I have needed to protect myself because when Australians are looking down the pointed finger of irresponsible politicians who are blaming the youth for more than 230 years of racism, more racism follows. Aboriginal people are profiled as criminals – all of us. Australians who should be our friends only see that finger pointing, their blinkers are on, and they get ignorant and they get angry. More harm is done.

The Indigenous population of youth in Australia are vibrant, colourful, courageous and the most loving people I have met. I think if Australia really wants to get to the bottom of this issue, they need to acknowledge the dark history which our people have endured and have been silenced for. Australia needs to listen and not reply, they need to open their minds but most importantly their hearts. We cannot change the past, but we can acknowledge it and we can make the future better by starting today, and this is why I love this book.

I may only be young, but I have already learnt that there are few people on this earth who have the emotional capacity to revisit the past and to articulately explain a path forward. Thomas Mayo is one of them.

In this book, Thomas conveys these subjects and matters with clarity and passion. He gives meaningful direction on how you can be an ally in a respectful and appropriate way.

As I delved into the pages I found it to be more than just an account of Aboriginal Australia's past; it's a moving story that exposes the injustices, hardships, and resilience of a people whose voices have been silenced for far too long.

These pages make us face hard realities regarding the past and present of our country. They emphasise the long-lasting effects of colonisation, such as the trauma passed down through generations, the gaps in wealth, and the loss of cultural identity. They serve as a reminder that the harm done to Indigenous communities is a continuous injustice that needs to be acknowledged and addressed, rather than seen as a relic from the past.

I dare to hope. I dare to speak up and ultimately, I dare you to take action. Start with this book.

Contents

Whether Yes or No, what's next?

In late December 2023, for the first time that year, I was with my family on the saltwater in my small dinghy. We were making numus from the fish we'd caught over the side. We were floating on Tiwi Country, on the border of Larrakia land.

On a build-up day like this, there's barely a whisper of wind. In the languages of the Torres Strait Islands, we call the sea's surface 'muthuru' when it lies still as it did that day, reflecting the sky like a mirror. While the scene is beautiful, in reality it is oppressively hot. Clouds give no relief from the heat of the sun, nor does the small canvas canopy on the boat. The humidity makes the air feel like hot soup.

Yet for all the uncomfortable heat, this is where I had longed to be as I travelled the country, working on the protracted and intense Voice to Parliament referendum campaign. Earlier that morning, my heart had swelled with pride as I watched my ten-year-old daughter Ruby hauling in a bunch of golden snappers. She's hardworking, a busy bee who grew so tall and lanky over the months when I was away. I noticed the chagrin of her twelve-year-old brother Will, who for all his bravado before the trip, had barely caught a fish.

A proper little Torres Strait Islander girl, Ruby shares my taste. She loves all things spicy and savoury and anything from the sea, and enjoys cooking, as I do. I asked her as I wrote this, 'What was your favourite part of fishing the other day?'

The first thing she said was, 'When we made the numus.'

Numus is raw fish and onion sliced thinly, with chopped birds-eye chillies and a dash of soya sauce. In a container in the esky, it cooks in the acidity of the other two ingredients – lemon juice and vinegar. In that fishing spot we always catch the best fish for the dish, a firm, white-fleshed fish called trevally. The numus is never better than when it is made fresh and eaten icy cold in the sweaty heat, accompanied by the scent of the salt air, and with family.

When I was a boy, I loved going to that same fishing spot with my father. It's a special place to me because, in a dinghy at sea, fishing and hunting, my father treated me differently from how he did at home. On land, he was much harsher.

My dad, Celestino Mayor, was part of a generation of Torres Strait Islander men who left their island home for the mainland to work – the first who could freely do so without interference from a white 'Protector' who could control every aspect of their lives. Dad was seventeen when he left Waiben on Kaurareg Country, otherwise known as Thursday Island.

Those Island men were famously hardworking. On 8 May 1968, a crew made up largely of Torres Strait Islanders broke the world record for laying the greatest length of railway track in one day.[1] Talk about heat and harsh conditions; they achieved that feat in the Pilbara, between Port Hedland and Mt Newman. Many of those men settled in mainland towns to raise their own families, as did my dad, while still sending money back to family on the islands.

I have strived to give my children the best things that my dad gave me – love, protection and a good example. I have consciously walked where he shone a light, rather than in his shadow. I have learnt from his mistakes and made my own, and I want my kids to learn from both of us, the good and the bad.

What I perceived as my father's flaws were as much about him preparing me for a world that did not love him. He rarely told me he loved me, believing that he needed to harden me up. He wanted me to be a man among men, no softness allowed, whereas I hold my kids close as often as they will let me; I tell them I love them every day.

Out there, in present-day Australia, sadly it feels as Noel Pearson described it in his 2022 Boyer Lectures:

> We are a much unloved people. We are perhaps the ethnic group Australians feel least connected to.
>
> We are not popular and we are not personally known to many Australians. Few have met us and a small minority count us as friends. And despite never having met any of us and knowing very little about us other than what is in the media and what WEH Stanner, whose 1968 Boyer Lectures looms large over my lectures, called 'folklore' about us – Australians hold and express strong views about us, the great proportion of which is negative and unfriendly.
>
> It has ever been thus. Worse in the past but still true today.[2]

Pearson is observing the majority of Australians' unfamiliarity with the First Peoples. When we do not know someone, we are easily misled to think the worst of them. Indeed, being much unloved is a hindrance to progress.

My approach to fatherhood has been to try to instil confidence and self-belief in my children – I want them to love themselves even if their country does not love them. I have tried this at every opportunity. Compared to my father's generation, and my generation, I want the next generation to live with less fear.

Perhaps it is this sentiment that has compelled me to write this book. I want you, who have a mind open enough to read it, to have the tools that you need – some lessons from the past and a guide for the future – so we can avoid a repeat of an outcome as sad as the referendum defeat. Together, we must bring on the next opportunity to take a major step toward justice for First Nations people.

Ultimately, we all should want to leave the next generation a little wiser, with a more peaceful, fairer world. This is the vision we fought for in 2023, and we will not lose sight of it. To achieve our goals for the future, we must take action.

Southerners rarely agree, but the Top End build-up is the best time of year in Darwin. The heat and humidity may be oppressive, as it was that day fishing, but there's the ice-cold numus to give us some relief and, like when we arrived back at the ramp at high tide, there is the wonderful tropical rain.

Since the referendum, I have enjoyed the mornings with our house open when it is cool, drinking a coffee while our kids get ready for school. Afterwards, I shut the louvres and turn on the aircon, waiting for the afternoon deluge. There's nothing better than sitting on the verandah reading a book as the heavens open, the lights flickering from the power of the storm. It has been nice to stay home and rest.

Now, however, it is early in the year after we lost the referendum. It is time for me to start writing again. Many of the 60,000 volunteers and the six million Australians who voted 'Yes' want to know what to do next. Some who voted 'No' still want progress.

Today, we may feel we are powerless to make the world what we want it to be – a world that has taken all possible measures to address the climate crisis; where the rich individuals and the grossly profitable companies pay their fair share of tax; where workers have strong enough rights to negotiate good wages, safe conditions and comfortable hours of work; a world where disputes can be resolved without war; a nation where Indigenous Australians can expect the same quality of life as our non-Indigenous friends.

In the wake of the referendum, versions of the same question have been posed by many of us: *What should we do next?*

Whether you voted 'Yes' or 'No', this book is for all those good people who have asked this question.

Within these pages are the ingredients for hope: energy, motivation and a belief in what you cannot yet see; you will find a guide to critical thinking, from the depths of the past to the truths and lies of the present; and a map, as practical as any tool I could give you, to see where the hazards are, the obstacles and the barriers and finally, a clear indication of how to reach our common destination: justice and recognition for Aboriginal and Torres Strait Islander people.

The campaign continues.

PART 1

Hope, resilience and motivations

I believe one cannot write about hope without using a personal perspective. So, a note before you start this Part: if you share my desire to see justice and recognition for Aboriginal and Torres Strait Islander people in our lifetimes, it does not matter if you are a worker or a boss, in the left faction or the right, or a footy fan but not into rugby. It doesn't even matter if at the last election you voted Liberal, Greens, Labor or Independent. What matters right now, in this very moment, is that you read the following chapters with an open mind and a readiness to feel what you cannot yet see.

CHAPTER 1

Hope

Hope is a necessary ingredient for change, and I believe that hope is contagious. This is why we start this book with a chapter about it, to try to understand how we can use and share hope to help achieve justice for Aboriginal and Torres Strait Islander people.

Hope is like energy. Sometimes we only have enough to survive day by day, with nothing left to give to others. Or we might have the energy to do more than just get by, we might have enough to do good in the world, if we so choose.

Motivation is another key ingredient to change. It can help us decide what we will choose to use our energy for, and how we will direct it.

If our hopes were only about ourselves – our personal pleasure and our profit – then the world would spiral into a scary place.

Whereas if we are motivated to do good for others, because we feel solidarity, empathy or love for them, and we share a desire for fairness, then we tend to listen, learn and act in their interest as well as our own, together.

If we cannot bring ourselves to believe that change is possible, then we may be in a state of hopelessness. Or we might have the energy but use it in destructive ways. That condition is just as contagious.

On the other hand, if we believe that we can eventually bring about change, then we can start to take the necessary steps to achieve that goal.

By the end of this book, I hope you will have the energy, motivation and, ultimately, the belief in what you can do to bring about positive change in the lives of First Nations people and for all Australians. I want you to have your own clearly defined hope for a better future.

My source of hope

When I reflect on the birth of my first child, I recognise a turning point in my life.

After a difficult delivery, my daughter came into the world covered in vernix – a pale, thick mucus, like the wrinkles on a wizened Elder. I stayed with mother and baby for as long as possible, then after kissing them goodnight, as I drove away from Darwin hospital, I hollered with joy and solemnly prayed to my ancestors that our daughter would live a full and healthy life.

Our baby's cheeks soon became full and chubby. Her hair thickened with tightly locked curls. Both her smile and her cry made my heart beat differently. Suddenly I understood hope in a new way.

I was barely twenty years old then, employed as a stevedore, also known as a wharfie, to load and unload ships. It was dangerous work, handling heavy machinery, equipment and cargoes. The cranes we used had the capacity to lift over 100 tonnes and they were many storeys high.

I was thrilled by the risks back then, excited to take on the challenging lifts, so heavy, using chains with links as thick as footballs.

But when my baby was born, followed by her sister and brother within three years, where previously I had barely noticed the dizzying heights, I began to feel fear.

I noticed that I would cringe at the eerie sounds of the steel structures as they bent toward the load on the hook and the depths of the sea. I began to feel every bump in my glass-floored cabin as it skipped across the boom of the gantry, parallel with the ground five storeys below.

I persevered. I still loved the work. But fatherhood seemed to shift my mindset to be more risk averse. I no longer looked forward to climbing the crane each shift. My thoughts changed from self-grandeur to warning of a plummeting doom.

When I think about what hope is, I think about the people I care about. What I choose to do in this world affects them. What I do today affects their tomorrow. They are where I get my energy from.

Politics matters

This newfound feeling of responsibility soon expanded when I learnt that politics matters. Politics is in everything we do, even when we choose to do nothing.

My definition of politics includes the activities of all law-makers, including governments, and how they are influenced. Politics is also someone's opinions about societal matters and how they use their opinions to influence others.

As well, politics is about relationships within a group or organisation that allow particular people to have power over others.

For some, let's call this group the 'Bad Actors', politics is their path, or their method, to achieve personal gain and power. Their goals may be to gain popularity, to feed their ego, or plain old greed to accumulate wealth.

Let's look at an example. The fossil fuel lobby and politicians who are financially supported by the fossil fuel industry might use political strategies to delay action on climate change. The highly paid lobbyists, who are often ex-politicians, the company shareholders and the top executives with their big bonuses have made billions of dollars between them during the many decades in which we have known that we could and should invest in a transition to clean energy. While this is happening, many Torres Strait Islanders who are losing their homes and lands to rising sea levels will be seriously harmed by the politics of the Bad Actors. But this is how decisions are being made in Australia and in many other nations.

For others, let's call this group the 'rest of us', participating in politics is to hope that everyone can share in the benefits that our society can offer. The rest of us want peace and prosperity for our families, but we don't want that to come at the cost of harming anyone else.

The more of us who are in this group, and who are well-informed, organised and active, the more power we will have. It's up to the rest of us to achieve justice for Aboriginal and Torres Strait Islander people, and to bring about changes that will help all of us have a better life.

Many good people are struggling in life – paying the bills, raising children, looking after their elders, trying to stay sane as the challenges roll in like waves in a relentless storm. They struggle to find the energy to hope, especially when suffering is becoming much more common at a global level. But when we work together – when we engage in politics in its broadest definition, supporting each other in our times of need – we give each other hope; and we are able to create the political power necessary for positive change.

Motivations

When I joined the union at the age of seventeen, I wasn't aware I was being political. I started at the port as a trainee, and while a couple of wharfies were teaching me how to drive the large forklifts, they told me about what the union had achieved over their long working lives. They politely suggested I join the union, the Maritime Union of Australia (MUA). They also told me about superannuation, advising that at my age especially, I should put a little extra in.

I had been taught to respect my elders, both Indigenous and non-Indigenous – a core value in First Nations culture. An Elder's experience is truly valued. I took their advice.

A formative experience for me on the wharves was the dispute between the Patrick Corporation (aka Patrick's), one of the two major stevedore companies in the country, and the MUA.

This landmark workplace dispute exploded in 1998 when Patrick's was backed by the Howard Coalition Government and the National Farmers Federation in an attempt to destroy the union.

In the middle of the night on 8 April, mercenaries, some wearing balaclavas, some with Rottweiler dogs straining at their leashes, physically dragged wharfies from their livelihoods in ports around the country, locking the gates behind them. The workers' employment was terminated through a dodgy human resources shuffle.[1]

Wharfies are traditionally a well-unionised part of the logistics chain, and for good reason. It is dangerous work and stevedore employers had treated their workers badly in the past. What was once a job that broke the backs of men for little pay, with no security of employment, had changed thanks to the strength of worker unity. By the time I stepped onto the wharf, there were permanent jobs with excellent pay and, when the ships were regular enough, with good rosters.

The lockout by Patrick's was an injustice that motivated hundreds of Australians to join the wharfies on picket lines at the port gates, as we fought to win our jobs back. After months of fighting, the union won the moral battle on the streets, and we won in the courts.

The Patrick's dispute broadened my imagination about hope. When our backs were against the wall, we seemed helpless. We were out the gate, on the bones of our arse, up against the government, the well-resourced employer and wealthy individuals. But politically, Australians saw our treatment as an injustice, and they came out in support.

We were a small workforce in Darwin. The old fellas, the leaders who had sacrificed so much to improve the conditions throughout decades, were to be made redundant but they wouldn't go unless their jobs remained as permanent positions, not lost to casualisation. They walked out the gates on strike one more time. It was this act of hope that delivered me a secure job.

Most of the men who replaced them were new to the wharf, and they were twice my age. They had no idea about standing up for each other, even so soon after the well-publicised dispute. Despite my quiet nature, I became a union delegate. I had learnt about protecting the interests of myself and my family by caring about the interests of others. So, a shy young man who barely said a word at work decided to step up to be a leader.

At this point, my world was the wharf, playing footy, fishing and family. I did not feel I was being political by being a delegate at work. It just had to be done. I wasn't going to let the sacrifices made by those union elders go to waste.

My Elders have remarked on how similar union culture is to Indigenous culture. We do things collectively as unions do. We also make decisions for the benefit of children several generations from now, not just for today.

When those old wharfies encouraged me to contribute extra to my superannuation, and I listened, they set me on course to one day retire with dignity – a full working life of savings with interest. But remarkably, the union elders who had convinced both employers and the government to guarantee superannuation for all Australians by going without pay on strikes – they were hard-fought negotiations – did so knowing that in the few years they had left in the workplace, they'd retire with little more than their final week's pay.

There are many rights that all Australians enjoy because of such collective acts of hope. Today, we take for granted that we have universal healthcare, personal leave and an expectation that we will not be killed in unsafe work environments. All of these social outcomes came about through workers in previous generations fighting for what they would hardly get to enjoy. Their hope and resilience – defying the Bad Actors who warned that each of the above reforms would destroy the economy – gave us much of what is good today.

ooooo

My first consciously political act beyond the workplace was to hand out how-to-vote cards for Kevin Rudd's Labor Party during the 2007 federal election. I was motivated by Prime Minster John Howard's poor record in Indigenous Affairs, and how his government had used their majority in the Senate and House of Representatives to introduce oppressive industrial relations laws, ironically called WorkChoices.

Soon after the legislation was passed on 10 November 2005, I had friends calling me in the middle of the night, whispering down the phone that they needed to see me. They would come to my place in tears, fearing they would lose their job if they were caught, or that they were breaking the law, just because they had sought advice about their pay and conditions. WorkChoices helped companies to employ staff on individual contracts and to minimise employment standards.

It didn't matter if a worker was a member of a union or not, nor how long they had been employed and if they had a good record of employment – they could be dismissed simply because someone else would do the job for lesser pay.[2] The new laws affected young and old. Grandparents worried about their grandchildren entering employment with few rights, so easily exploited by unscrupulous employers.

As well as trying to destroy my union in the 1998 Patrick's dispute, John Howard's government set us back decades in Indigenous affairs. They took away ATSIC (Aboriginal and Torres Strait Islander Commission), an effective representative body that was improving housing, employment and leadership in Indigenous communities. And they suspended the *Racial Discrimination Act* in 2007 to introduce a heinous policy – the Northern Territory Emergency Response, otherwise known as 'The Intervention' (read more about this in Part Two).

On 24 November 2007, Labor resoundingly won the federal election, and John Howard lost his own seat of Bennelong, becoming only the second Prime Minister to lose his own seat after Stanley Bruce in 1929.

In that election campaign, thousands of people across so many parts of our society came together because they saw the need for change. We shared our hopes and built on each other's energy, and we changed the government.

Resilience against hopelessness

In early 2023, after more than two centuries of genocide, dispossession and exclusion, and a widening gap between Indigenous and non-Indigenous people in the past decade, a majority of Indigenous

Australians dared hope we would have a permanent place at the decision-making table. We thought we might finally be recognised in the Australian Constitution. But instead, during the referendum campaign, we found ourselves on trial, expected to answer for all the wrongs against us, as if we were the perpetrators of crimes we did not commit.

I will discuss the tactics that Bad Actors use and how their friends in the media reliably amplify their negative spin in Part Three. But here I want to mention the importance of resilience and how it relates to hope.

Politics is an eternal tug-o-war. Left and right. Right and wrong. Us and them. Positive and negative. Negative, negative, negative. This is one of the reasons that Australians tend to be disengaged from it. Bad Actors want us to disengage, to not care enough, to give up and focus on ourselves without pursuing the truth. They want us to be so polarised that we cannot discuss politics at the kitchen table.

We need to build a resilience to the discomfort we feel when we discuss political matters. Then we can talk with our friends and family about matters that we believe are important for our whole country.

ooooo

During the referendum campaign, I was a national scapegoat.

The No campaign took their first swipe at me through the Murdoch media, with a full page of mashed together quotes – things I had said throughout almost a decade of activism. The quotes were indeed ideas I had talked about, even supported during the shaping of my personal political beliefs, and as Aboriginal and Torres Strait Islander people negotiated our way forward.

'Pay the rent', 'reparations', 'tearing down the institutions that harm us' – shocking, isn't it, that a people so wronged would discuss such ideas?

There were many instances when I made speeches at rallies for justice. Was I supposed to politely sing 'Advance Australia Fair' among aggrieved families following another death in custody, or when another young Indigenous person was put in jail?

Snip a clip from an impassioned speech here, extract a quote from a debate there, present it all together, and there you have it – the scary Black man trope.

Going back over my years of passionate advocacy, they found all they needed to present the angry Black man who is here to take your backyard. They made me the stereotype: a militant union thug, a communist who hates Australia. The only truth in that is that I am a member and leader of a union, and I'm proud of that.

Soon after, an official No campaign full-page advertisement was printed in the *Australian Financial Review*. It depicted a caricature of me wearing raggedy jeans and a red shirt with a communist logo on it, dancing a jig for money.

The Bad Actors brought me to my lowest moment in the campaign. I contemplated quitting. It was hard to think clearly, and I was sorely missing home. I felt like I no longer had any energy for others.

Many other Indigenous leaders who stepped up to support the Voice experienced this. So did non-Indigenous supporters who were harassed online and at market stalls, mentally slapped around to get an angry reaction that could be splashed across the media.

I share this because we must insulate our hope against the Bad Actors' tactics of intimidation that will be used again and again. They will try to bully us into silence, to find ways to sever support from the public, and on social media especially, they will use trolls to make each of us feel alone.

The way to deal with this type of intimidation is to double down on our loud, proud support for what we believe is right. We should not be cowed to soften our stance when what we are working towards is justice.

When I was unfairly represented in the media, I was saddened by the personal nature of the attacks – especially by how the No campaign was dishonestly poisoning a rare opportunity for meaningful Indigenous recognition.

I did not give up. Instead, I worked harder. Day and night, seven days a week I fought on for our children who are being taken from their families, for Indigenous people who are dying in custody, to change a system that ignores their trauma and the racism that confronts them, not just in the streets, but also in the power structures of their nation.

I say we should use hope and resilience to build a fire in our bellies. Whatever the Bad Actors throw at us, let it burn to give us energy.

I ask that non-Indigenous people try to understand our anger when we protest. For my fellow Indigenous people, we should use our anger to be heard. But we should temper our anger – hone the edge of our rage into a key that will open hearts and minds, rather than a blade that will sever our support.

The Uluṟu Statement from the Heart was a call for peace. The Voice, a means for discussion.

When my children were born, I felt their vulnerability, and it made me want to live for them. When I was learning about politics, I was discovering that the best way to live for them was to actively hope with like-minded people, because protecting their children protected mine too. We experienced a loss at the referendum, but we gained resilience, and I refuse to give up my hope – a new generation of Indigenous leaders are ready.

Hope!

When we have hope, we can heal, as exercise awakens lost muscle. Hope is how we learn. If we don't take action, if we never try, we won't know how to lose, and then we will never understand how we can win.

Think about the struggle we've had toward justice for Aboriginal and Torres Strait Islander people thus far. From 100 per cent of the population to near annihilation, where are we today?

Today, Indigenous groups have Native Title and land rights covering large swathes of the nation. Traditional Owners have been able to use these rights to negotiate outcomes that will protect our Country, and by negotiating ongoing benefits through Indigenous Land Use Agreements.

From an impressive all-Aboriginal cricket team in the late 19th century, to Lionel Rose, Evonne Goolagong, Michael Long, Cathy Freeman, Andrew McLeod, Patrick Mills, big Arty Beetson, and so many others in sport; to Archie Roach, Yothu Yindi, Troy Cassar-Daley, Christine Anu, Emma Donovan, Dan Sultan, Briggs, Barkaa and the King Stingray band in music – the list goes on in a cascade of stars across our southern sky.

We have seen an ever-expanding diversity of Indigenous academics and scholars. Aboriginal and Torres Strait Islander people are practising law and becoming silks and judges, running lucrative businesses, leading their unions, writing and illustrating books, and winning elections to represent us in Parliament.

When I was a child, I don't think there were any Aboriginal or Torres Strait Islander doctors, but as of 2021, according to reports from the Indigenous-led Australian Indigenous Doctors' Association (AIDA), there were 519.[3]

Each of these achievers across all the areas they excel in have overcome prejudice and racism to become who they are, and each of them inspires hope for the next generation.

When our Elders first sought a right to vote, we were told No. When we first demanded equal wages, the answer was No. When we first marched and litigated for land rights and Native Title, they said No. In 2023, when we called for a Voice in the Constitution, we received that familiar response – No.

Why do we have hope?

Because every time we were told No, we took action with non-Indigenous allies. We got that fire in our bellies. And here we are now, on the field winning games, in the boardrooms leading change, in the concert halls filling seats to capacity, in the universities lecturing, and in the Parliaments, representing all Australians. We are here to stay, and we say 'No' does not mean 'No to progress'. We always were and always will be for 'Yes'.

Compared to fifty years ago, we have come a long way. But we still have a long way to go. The statistics – the reality on the ground in many Indigenous communities, in the prison cells and on the hospital beds – are a crying shame. Our gains are under attack.

If you are walking with us, we must find our energy and give hope to others. If you are First Nations, continue to be loud and proud; fight for your rights with the commitment and determination of your ancestors.

Why have I written this book? The answer begins with the love of my family, community and fellow Australians.

Why are you reading this book? The answer is that you care.

Together, we have hope.

CHAPTER 2

What about the Uluru Statement from the Heart now?

The day after the referendum, Sunday 15 October, I awoke in Sydney with an aching emptiness in my chest. I packed my suitcase and dragged it with the broken pieces of my heart to a hotel by the sea in Coogee.

I'd been home for only twenty-five days across the year up till that point. Nevertheless, my wife and I had agreed to a plan: whatever the result, I would immediately write an article or essay about what was next. We both know that I'm not really present when I'm writing to a tight deadline, so we decided that I may as well stay in Sydney another week on my own.

The nearby cold saltwater was perfect for washing away writer's block; within a week I had articulated my thoughts in an article to be published in the next *The Saturday Paper* and I had almost completed an essay for *Meanjin Quarterly*. The job done, I headed home to Darwin.

They say distance makes the heart grow fonder, and I felt it. My pent-up emotions, so turbulent, were flooded with little else but love when I stepped off the plane and into the arms of my family. I am a father of five kids, three in their twenties, and the youngest two were ten and twelve years old then. In my family's eyes, I returned a hero – somehow even my oldest kids found my dad jokes funny.

In my ponderings during November and December, I thought I would never recite the Uluṟu Statement from the Heart again. During the campaign, I had presented it with my heart on my sleeve, with every ounce of persuasiveness I could muster, hoping I was building the empathy and understanding Australians would need to resist the dark lies about us and vote 'Yes'. With the outcome of the referendum in my mind, I just couldn't imagine reciting it again.

In January 2024, I started writing this book and later that month I travelled interstate to a conference to deliver my first speech for the year. In the briefing beforehand, I was asked if I would recite the Uluṟu Statement at the close of the talk. I explained why I wouldn't, how I felt too rejected, too hurt, too empty, but then I changed my mind.

The Uluṟu Statement from the Heart is no less true because of the referendum result. The need for a Voice is no less logical, no less important. It remains the best way to design policies and laws, giving a Voice to the people who they affect most.

It also remains the most powerful public document that anyone in this nation has ever produced. It is the only national public statement endorsed by a consensus of Indigenous peoples – by tracking the 'Yes' votes across the country, it is irrefutable that the Uluṟu Statement is supported by a majority of Indigenous Australians. Many people still feel the words are more moving than anything they have read or heard in their lives, and I feel this way myself.

At the conference in January, I recited the Uluṟu Statement with a slight change to say that a Voice remains important, though sure, it wouldn't be added to the Australian Constitution any time soon. The words were heavy in my throat but saying them out loud to this gathering felt like an act of defiance – a statement calling for peace, not war, as the No campaign claimed in their unrelenting fight against it.

The room stood as one, as Aboriginal and Torres Strait Islander people did in the heart of the nation on 26 May 2017 when Professor Megan Davis read it aloud for the first time. People cried, as we had done at the Uluṟu Convention, and as so many Australians did when we shared those words in meetings and rallies in 2023. A superficial 'No' cannot override such heartfelt hope.

I say to all who will listen, read the Uluṟu Statement from the Heart. Share it. Teach your children about it. Put it up on your wall. Commit to walk with us, for Voice, Treaty, Truth, as it invites you to do. It continues to be a call to action from Aboriginal and Torres Strait Islander people to this nation.

Uluṟu Statement from the Heart

We, gathered at the 2017 National Constitutional Convention, coming from all points of the southern sky, make this statement from the heart:

Our Aboriginal and Torres Strait Islander tribes were the first sovereign Nations of the Australian continent and its adjacent islands, and possessed it under our own laws and customs. This our ancestors did, according to the reckoning of our culture, from the Creation, according to the common law from 'time immemorial', and according to science more than 60,000 years ago.

This sovereignty is *a spiritual notion: the ancestral tie between the land, or 'mother nature', and the Aboriginal and*

Torres Strait Islander peoples who were born therefrom, remain attached thereto, and must one day return thither to be united with our ancestors. This link is the basis of the ownership of the soil, or better, of sovereignty. It has never been ceded or extinguished, and co-exists with the sovereignty of the Crown.

How could it be otherwise? That peoples possessed a land for sixty millennia and this sacred link disappears from world history in merely the last two hundred years?

With substantive constitutional change and structural reform, we believe this ancient sovereignty can shine through as a fuller expression of Australia's nationhood.

Proportionally, we are the most incarcerated people on the planet. We are not an innately criminal people. Our children are aliened from their families at unprecedented rates. This cannot be because we have no love for them. And our youth languish in detention in obscene numbers. They should be our hope for the future.

These dimensions of our crisis tell plainly the structural nature of our problem. This is *the torment of our powerlessness.*

We seek constitutional reforms to empower our people and take *a rightful place* in our own country. When we have power over our destiny our children will flourish. They will walk in two worlds and their culture will be a gift to their country.

We call for the establishment of a First Nations Voice enshrined in the Constitution.

Makarrata is the culmination of our agenda: *the coming together after a struggle.* It captures our aspirations for a fair and truthful relationship with the people of Australia and a better future for our children based on justice and self-determination.

We seek a Makarrata Commission to supervise a process of agreement-making between governments and First Nations and truth-telling about our history.

In 1967 we were counted, in 2017 we seek to be heard. We leave base camp and start our trek across this vast country. We invite you to walk with us in a movement of the Australian people for a better future.[1]

26 May 2017

PART 2

Learning from the past

In the following chapters, I write about aspects of our First Nations' history, to help us understand the situation today and decide what we must do next. Some of what I share here will be sad and confronting, especially after we have just explored hope. I want you to feel these emotions though, before you read Part Three, which is about taking action. Let what you feel in Part Two put that fire in your belly. Let this part be a source of motivation.

Please note that this is not intended to be a detailed, academic view of the last 250 years or the past 65,000 years. There are many excellent works that delve into our history, and some are listed in the 'Useful resources' pages at the end of this book. Instead, I focus on particular events and ideas that I believe are important to remember and talk about, and attitudes that are based on a narrow view of Australia's history that we should question and revise.

CHAPTER 3

Always was – the first 65,000 years

O ur country has much more than a mere two and a half centuries of human history – civilisation on this continent stretches back more than 65,000 years. This statement is a core truth and should not be regarded as contentious.

To understand that Australia always was and always will be Aboriginal and Torres Strait Islander land, we can listen to our Elders. They are part of a line that stretches back, according to the reckoning of our culture, to the creation. For countless generations, the First Peoples diligently and accurately passed on the lessons from the past, developing our unique and vibrant cultures.

Feeling, seeing and believing

You will find accounts of our history in books and documentaries, although nothing beats hearing the stories directly from our Elders, as they first heard them, while feeling the earth under your feet and the warmth of a fire, as the ancestors watch on from the stars. These stories contain the most important lessons about life – how we love, how temptations and jealousy can lead one astray, about responsibility, sustainability, and respect for each other and for all living things and for Country itself.

The Seven Sisters is one such story that has been carried throughout millennia.

As with any great story, there are various interpretations depending on one's perspective, or the lessons that are being taught. The Seven Sisters story, broadly speaking, is about a group of women who came from afar to walk the vastness of the land. It tells of adventure, love, and a drama that shaped the features of our country. The tale culminates in a man, infatuated by one of the sisters who lingered on the earth, following her into the night sky. There are some parts of the story that are sacred to certain groups and cannot be told to others. Under the southern sky though, we share the Seven Sisters symbol, more commonly known as the Southern Cross.

Another story is about Buladjang or 'Sickness Country'. It comes from the Jawoyn people in the Top End, and it holds lessons for all of us today when we consider the dangers associated with uranium mining. The story starts with the Bula spirit, who walked south from the coast of the Northern Territory, bringing his wives with him. As he walked and hunted on the land, he created the landscape.

Other creation ancestors joined him. They included gupu (plains kangaroo or antilopine wallaroo), barrk (black wallaroo), garrkayn (brown goshawk), belerrk (gecko lizard), ngarratj (white cockatoo), and bolung (the rainbow serpent). Bula's image is seen in paintings in rock shelters, and his spirit is in the earth in parts of the South Alligator Valley in the Northern Territory.

The Jawoyn people protect this Country still today. They are responsible for preventing disturbances that could upset Bula and cause universal destruction. They famously succeeded in 1992, after

a long struggle, to convince Prime Minister Bob Hawke to stop a
uranium mine from going ahead at Coronation Hill.[1]

There are countless stories like these, often linked across many
thousands of kilometres. In English they are described as Songlines
for the way they are connected, and how they have been preserved
and communicated.

You can appreciate this wealth of history and knowledge by looking
at the many and diverse First Nations artworks in museums and
galleries around Australia and in collections overseas. And you can
feel the true story of precolonial Australia when you are on Country,
in that special place.

Think about how you felt when you first reached that green valley
covered in yellow and purple wildflowers; or the beach by the deep
blue sea fringed by white surf and silver fish playing in the shallows.
Do you remember that waterhole, tucked into the folds of a red rock,
surrounded by an ocean of ochre; or those wetlands, reflecting a
brilliant orange and purple dusk as magpie geese foraged at the foot
of an ancient escarpment? In those moments, you felt the idyllic life
that Indigenous people enjoyed in this great country.

The next time you are in that special Australian place, take the time
to acknowledge what a peaceful and abundant life Aboriginal and
Torres Strait Islander people lived. Think about the ways they cared
for those places, using their wisdom handed down from the ancestors.

Take a really hard look. Suspend any prejudice and preconceptions.
Imagine how the children would have dived for mussels and played in
the rainbow spray from that waterfall; or slid down those dunes
during the cool mornings and made dolls from native grasses for play
in the afternoon shade; or just lain in the sun by the river, with their
bellies full of fish and wild yams, the familiar smell of smoke and the
comforting sound of their mothers laughing, suckling their youngest

child, cooing, as the men excitedly spun a yarn about how their totem appeared at dawn, guiding their great catch.

Captain James Cook observed Indigenous life as it was before his 'discovery' ushered in a dark age of destruction. In the journal of HMS *Endeavour*, 1768–71, Cook wrote:

> From what I have said of the Natives of New Holland they may appear to some to be the most wretched people upon earth, but in reality they are far more happier than we Europeans; being wholly unacquainted not only with the superfluous but necessary Conveniences so much sought after in Europe, they are happy in not knowing the use of them. They live in a Tranquility which is not disturb'd by the Inequality of the Condition.[2]

Finally, you could listen to the science.

In 2020, at the Yirra site in the Pilbara, Western Australia, artefacts were found that were more than 50,000 years old. Peter Veth, Professor of Archaeology at the University of Western Australia, said, 'I think it is very likely that Yirra and other desert places will eventually prove to be up to 60,000 years old – that's before modern humans get to Europe. It's a unique global record.'[3]

The Warratyi site[4] in the Flinders Ranges, South Australia, is estimated to be around 49,000 years old. Located about 550 km north of Adelaide, it is a rock shelter and contains evidence of humans' interactions with megafauna. Professor Gavin Prideaux, from Flinders University, co-authored a paper published in *Nature*[5] about the site. He said that the 2016 paper 'smashed several paradigms about Indigenous Australians'. 'People … were set up in arid southern Australia by about 50,000 years ago and they had all these amazing technologies much earlier than we thought.'[6]

The oldest site for human habitation so far documented is Madjedbebe, near Kakadu National Park in the Northern Territory. It is a sandstone rock shelter where scientists have uncovered artefacts that are around 65,000 years old. Associate Professor in Archaeology, Dr Chris Clarkson, from the School of Social Science at the University of Queensland, was the lead author of a paper in the journal *Nature*, which is extremely interesting.[7] He said that the science demonstrates a strong cultural continuity across thousands of years. 'The fundamental aspects of technology, such as axes, grindstones and the production of ochre to produce art goes from the present right the way [back].

'It suggests there is a very, very deep continuity and connection between the people living in Kakadu today and probably those living there 65,000 years ago.'[8]

The artefacts include ground-edge axes and the world's oldest-known grinding-stone, which is evidence of the local Indigenous people's seed grinding and intensive plant use.

We were experts at making peace

Our continent cradled an advanced civilisation with hundreds of First Nations' cultures. Intrinsic to how Aboriginal and Torres Strait Islander people expressed their values, beliefs and customs, and key to keeping knowledge about Country, were the almost 800 languages that they used.

Currently, all of these languages are in a critical and precarious state.[9] A few are learnt by children as their first language, some are a regular medium of communication, some are sleeping, and many are being reawakened by their community custodians.

The critical state of Aboriginal and Torres Strait Islander languages should be an urgent matter for all of us. They are irreplaceable and invaluable. To see the language groups around the country, I recommend you explore the Gambay – First Languages Map, produced by First Languages Australia.[10]

For so many unique languages to evolve on one continent, it logically follows that Indigenous peoples were masters at dispute resolution. Compared to Europe, where feudalism and conquest raged through the 'dark ages' and beyond to the invasions of Indigenous peoples across the globe in the past several centuries, Aboriginal and Torres Strait Islander people enjoyed relative peace.

I'm not saying there wasn't violence. There were wars and feuds. But First Nations had strict protocols and laws to minimise bloodshed.[11] They achieved peace through cultures that valued mutual respect, honesty, fairness and an understanding of one's place in society and in the land – a recognition that we belong to the land as much as the land belongs to us.

An example of a First Nations peace-making process is Makarrata. This is a Yolŋu word that is briefly translated in the Uluṟu Statement as a 'coming together after a struggle'.

The late Dr Yunupingu wrote:

> The Principles of Makarrata have guided Yolŋu people in North East Arnhem Land through difficult disputes for centuries and they are useful as a guide to the current challenge.
>
> First, the disputing parties must be brought together. Then, each party, led by their elders must speak carefully and calmly about the dispute. They must put the facts on the table and air their grievances. If a person speaks wildly, or out of turn, he or she is sent away and shall not be included any further in the process. Those who come for vengeance or for no other purposes, will also be sent away, for they can only disrupt the process.
>
> The leaders must always seek a full understanding of the

dispute: what lies behind it; who is responsible; what each party wants; and all things that are normal to peacemaking efforts. When that understanding is arrived at, then a settlement can be agreed upon. This settlement is also a symbolic reckoning – an action that says to the world that from now on and forever the dispute is settled; that the dispute no longer exists, it is finished. And from the honesty of the process and the submission of both parties to finding the truth, then the dispute is ended. In past times a leader came forward and accepted a punishment and this leader once punished was then immediately taken into the heart of the aggrieved clan. The leader's wounds were healed by the men and women of the aggrieved clan, and the leader was given gifts and shown respect – and this former foe, who had caused pain and suffering to people, would live with those that had been harmed and the peace was made – not just for them but for future generations.

In this way the parties were able to come together, to trade, to marry, to work together and make their lives together. The dispute was over and peace and harmony were achieved.[12]

From time to time, you may meet or read commentary from someone who believes that Indigenous people's ways were, and continue to be, especially violent.

Historically, First Nations laws were no more violent than the European laws, with their guillotines, hangings, crucifixions, not to mention all manner of cruel torture.

It is true to say that Indigenous people were demonstrably less violent.

In Aboriginal and Torres Strait Islander culture, no living being was incarcerated – neither animal nor human. The most feared punishment in Aboriginal society was not the death penalty but being exiled by your community from your Country and your family to live in shame.

Why have Australians been taught that Indigenous people were violent savages and unintelligent, in need of saving by the European forefathers of this nation?

If Australians believe that the original occupants were primitive, less than animals, not worthy of empathy, then they will believe there was no genocide, no need for reparative actions, and the power structures that make it so easy to use us as scapegoats will stay intact.

Our culture is steeped in ancient wisdom, and it is evolving as any culture does. Our ways could be as harsh as any civilisation's more than 200 years ago, and yet they were also often gentle and fair. Our forebears were intelligent, innovative, inventive and scientific.

We were once remarkably peaceful and happy, and we want that for our children today.

Who we were before remains who we are now. We never needed saving. We always deserved justice.

CHAPTER 4

Always will be – a long history of injustice

From the arrival of the First Fleet to the Coniston massacre in the Northern Territory in 1928, this chapter touches on just some of the cruel injustices that our people faced from the earliest days of British invasion and colonisation.

The First Fleet landed on the shores of the Eora nation on 18 January 1788, under the charge of Governor Arthur Phillip. Eleven ships carrying around 1400 people – government officials, military, tradesmen and their families, and about 700 convicts – stopped in the area later known as Botany Bay. They then moved north to what they decided was the more suitable area of Sydney Cove on 26 January, where they established the first European settlement.

Prior to this, Europeans had sailed to this country but didn't stay long. The Dutch had briefly visited our continent several times in the seventeenth century. Interactions with Cook had been eighteen years before the arrival of the First Fleet. It is likely that the people of the Eora nation let the British fish and hunt unimpeded because they expected that the visitors would do as others had done and soon move on.

During the first twelve months of the settlement, the Indigenous people were patient with these new arrivals; the initial interactions were mostly amicable and curious. The Brits made sure to quickly demonstrate their firepower, giving demonstrations of what their guns could do to a wooden shield. But people from the local area, the Gadigal, and the nearby nations and beyond outnumbered the British and could have overwhelmed them. This approach shows that Aboriginal people were not the violent savages that generations of Australians have been led to believe.

By contrast, could you imagine what the response would have been if an armed, foreign party had arrived by ship somewhere along the English coastline in 1788? Or what would happen if a contingent landed today at Circular Quay, with an unknown language, foreign ways, advanced weaponry, and an air of superiority, thinking themselves beyond reproach?

The first years of the invasion

Cook's botanist on the *Endeavour*, Sir Joseph Banks, championed the case for convicts to be sent to this country through the House of Commons parliamentary committee on convicts in 1779. His testimony, recorded by the committee, seriously demeaned First Nations people:

> He apprehended there would be little probability of any opposition from the natives, as during his stay there in the year 1770 he saw very few, and did not think there were above fifty in all the neighbourhood, and had reason to believe the country was thinly peopled; those he saw were naked, treacherous, and armed with lances, but extremely cowardly, and constantly retired from our people when they made the least appearance of resistance.[1]

Contrary to Banks' report, Aboriginal warriors, who were far more appropriately attired than the colonisers, and loyal to their Country, armed with spears and shields, were endeavouring to protect the women and children, and uphold the nations' laws.

ooooo

After about a year of occupation, Governor Arthur Phillip was becoming frustrated with the slow expansion of the colony. His intelligence on the Aboriginal population was poor, and it was clear that they were in greater numbers and had greater capability than he had been led to believe before leaving Britain.

Apart from brief gatherings, the owners of the land wanted little to do with the British. This frustrated Phillip's attempts to gather information about them and establish an exchange of language. So he decided to take a radical new approach to Indigenous relations. He intended to force Aboriginal people to share vital information and convert them to British ways, so they could go forth and spread the word on just how wonderful those British ways were. To do this, Phillip ordered a violent kidnapping. Now there's a lesson in diplomacy.

The first man they abducted was named Arabanoo.[2] On 31 December 1788, a small party of soldiers coaxed him to come close to their boat in waters in the area now known as Manly, and threw a rope around his neck, dragging him into captivity.

Arabanoo was described as a gentle man who was immediately homesick. It was recorded that he was shocked when he saw convicts being flogged. Aboriginal justice did not involve having people bound and beaten, unable to defend themselves. He shared some language and learnt some English, but died on 18 May 1789 from smallpox during a devastating outbreak.

Around half of the people of the Aboriginal population in the region died from the disease, according to Indigenous witnesses at the time.[3] The epidemic was horrific. British sailors reported seeing bodies strewn on the beaches and floating in the water. The epidemic dampened resistance to the British.

As the British tendrils reached across the continent, in some instances, Aboriginal and Torres Strait Islander people did not realise they were being invaded.[4] Around the country, some believed that the newcomers were the white-faced ghosts of ancestors returning.[5] This makes sense when you consider how few and far between the visits of white people had been.

In the Torres Strait Islands we call these white ghosts 'Markai'. Australian author Ion Idriess wrote about such an encounter in his 1933 novel, *Drums of Mer*, which he said was based on a true story. Two boys from a shipwrecked crew were warmly greeted by Islanders because they resembled the deceased sons of the chief.

When white 'explorers' or shipwrecked sailors were thought to be a lost son or daughter reincarnated, they were received with tears of joy and lovingly embraced. It's sad to think they might have 'reintroduced' imposters to Country, the waterholes, the hunting grounds, the areas of fertile soils and shelters, only to have that knowledge used to dispossess them.

With Arabanoo dead, Phillip sent out another kidnapping party that captured two more warriors. Their names were Colebee and Bennelong.

Colebee soon escaped incarceration at Sydney Cove, but Bennelong remained.

He may have stayed so he could learn about the colony. You could imagine there were many questions that the people of the area were asking, such as about the origin of the diseases, the intent of the foreigners, and in particular how long they planned to stay. The answers could be a matter of life and death.

Bennelong, a Wangal man, was said to have been charismatic and sharply intelligent.[6] He was quick to learn to communicate effectively, and developed a relationship with Governor Phillip, though his captors kept him in fetters. By April 1790, he had gained enough trust to be unbound, and then he promptly escaped.

The next time Bennelong and Phillip met marks a rare moment when the colonisers accepted Indigenous law – though they were still deliberately blind to their sovereignty.

In 1790, at Bennelong's invitation, he and Phillip with their respective parties met at Kyeemy, or Manly Cove as the British called it, where they shared some whale meat. During this meeting, Phillip was speared. The weapon was around three metres long but did not have multiple barbs and the like that would have been used if the intention were to kill. The person who threw it, a Kadaitcha man, with the lawful and spiritual authority to deliver such ritual justice, aimed true, wounding Phillip in the shoulder.

The punishment could have been for multiple breaches of Aboriginal law: the kidnapping of Arabanoo, Colebee and Bennelong; the desecration of land and water sources; the exploitation of animals without due process or proper respect; no doubt the list could go on. To the Aboriginal people, it was likely about a leader taking responsibility for his tribe's wrongdoings, that is, Phillip on behalf of his colony, an atonement without death. In Aboriginal law, an act such as the spearing was a way to return balance, foster new friendships and bring about peace. When you consider that in those times, serious breaches of British law could have resulted in utterly miserable solitary confinement, death by multiple wounds from a firing squad, or being exiled in chains to the other side of the globe, the Aboriginal response was civilised in comparison.

Phillip seemed to understand the intent of the spearing and relations were reset with a short period of peace. Bennelong moved into the settlement, sharing his culture and language with the British. He also went to England before his passing in 1813. He learnt enough in Britain to come to the conclusion that 'there was no better country than his own and that he did not wish to leave it'.[7]

While the Governor's response may have seemed reasoned, the British had one unwavering intent. Their expansion would not be halted.

Headhunters

The ships of the Second Fleet were loaded with sick and dying convicts who had been confined in chains below decks. More than a quarter had died onboard and more would die soon after they landed.

Imagine what the peaceful and civilised Aboriginal people would have thought when the ships approached and the convicts were brought ashore. The putrid smell. The sickness. The cruelty. The horror.

Also on the Second Fleet was a letter from Sir Joseph Banks to Phillip, requesting he send him 'native' heads. Banks' extraordinary level of influence was evident in the Governor's response. 'I shall send skulls by the *Gorgon*,' Phillip wrote on 26 July 1790. 'I shall always be happy in receiving your commands.'[8]

The opportunity to gratify Banks presented itself in December that year, when Phillip's favoured game-shooter John McIntyre was fatally speared by a formidable warrior called Pemulwuy.

The senior military officer at Sydney Cove, Captain Watkin Tench, believed that this was no random attack and that McIntyre had given serious offence to the First Nations people. He said of McIntyre:

'From the aversion uniformly shewn by all natives to this unhappy man, he had long been suspected by us of having on his excursions shot and injured them …'[9] Tench had also noted that Bennelong regarded McIntyre with 'much dread and hatred'.

Governor Phillip insisted the attack was unprovoked, and so he instructed Tench to lead an expedition of fifty marines and two surgeons to Botany Bay, some 12 kilometres south of Sydney Cove. Their mission was to capture two Indigenous men for a public execution in Sydney and to kill and take the heads of ten more.

Shocked at this, Tench tried to reason with Phillip but was only able to reduce the head requirement from ten to six. He set off at dawn on 14 December, carrying hatchets for decapitation and bags for the heads.[10] When the party finally reached Botany Bay, they failed to capture any Aboriginal men for decapitation. Back they trudged to Sydney Cove, only to be ordered out again.

On his second attempt, Tench sought the element of surprise and instructed his guides to find the quickest route, which led through a swampy area they thought might be negotiable, but it proved not to be. Tench's party almost perished in thick mud, like quicksand, crossing a creek. Badly shaken, they continued to march to another site where Aboriginal people lived. 'To our astonishment,' Tench recorded, 'we found not a single native at the huts; nor was a canoe to be seen on any part of the bay.'[11] Rather than teach the Aboriginal people a lesson about European superiority, Phillip's early punitive expeditions were an utter folly. 'A most tedious march as ever men went in the time,' as one exhausted soldier observed.[12]

It is likely that Bennelong or others in the settlement had alerted the local Aboriginal people so they could stay ahead of Tench. However, future murderous missions under subsequent governors did not fail.

In response to the Governor's overreach, Bidjigal man Pemulwuy rose up as a fearless warrior for his people. For years afterwards, he coordinated a daring campaign that effectively curtailed the spread of the colonial settlement.

The escalation of the Frontier Wars

By now, it was becoming abundantly clear that the very existence of the colony was dependent on a regime of violence against First Nations people.

To the west of Sydney, in the fertile river lands of the Burramattagal clan of the Dharug nation, the British established their first inland settlement, along with government farms that were vital to supporting a growing population of colonists. The violations of Aboriginal land and First Nations law became more frequent and widespread. It's important to note that settlers and British authorities often broke their own laws as well. I discuss this in chapter 8.

From 1792, Pemulwuy led his warriors in guerrilla warfare across Bidjigal lands, punishing law breakers, strategically burning buildings, taking crops and attacking travellers.[13] At the height of these raids, in March 1797, he and 100 warriors fought in what has become known as the Battle of Parramatta against armed soldiers and settlers. During the fighting, Pemulwuy was shot in the head and body.

He was treated in the Parramatta hospital until he was thought well enough to be hanged, although his wounds were so bad, he was not expected to survive. The decision to hang Pemulwuy would most likely have been to make an example of him, to deter others from standing up for their people. Miraculously, he escaped while still bound in irons, and although seriously injured he continued to fight for his Country, seemingly immune to the white man's guns.

In 1801, the third governor of the colony, Philip Gidley King, issued a general order that Aboriginal people near Parramatta and Prospect could be shot on sight.[14] A set of rewards were offered for Pemulwuy's head, the most enticing of which was '20 gallons of spirits'. A settler eager to claim the reward shot the great warrior dead on 2 June 1802. He was decapitated and his head sent to Sir Joseph Banks in England, who donated it to his friend Dr John Hunter, for his skull collection.[15]

Pemulwuy was one of many heroes who defended their Country. For decades now, First Nations people have been calling for the return of stolen land, Pemulwuy's stolen skull, and many other stolen bodies and their material property.

Lest we forget the warriors of the resistance.

ooooo

The first 200 years of white Australian history were rife with violence against Aboriginal and Torres Strait Islander people. Yes, there was violence against the colonisers as well, of course there was. First Nations people were defending their Country from invasion, acting in accordance with their well-established laws. Defending the heritage, culture and ways of life as passed on by your forebears is what humans have done forever.

In Australia, our First Nations' resistance is known as the Frontier Wars. While there were flashes of courageous allyship and friendship from white people, there were too few who stood with us, and when they did, it was always on the coloniser's terms. When Aboriginal and Torres Strait Islander people killed white settlers, the response was extreme, with disproportionately more Aboriginal men, women and children killed, and often in far more gruesome ways.

The sum of every act of the invading British settlers was still genocide: to clear Indigenous people from the land for colonial settlement. Those who were spared were forcibly removed to reserves

to languish in poverty, or used like slaves. Indigenous people were
subjected to forced assimilation, where speaking their own language,
for example, led to cruel punishments such as beatings and children
being forced to rake a yard with their bare hands. And it was all
justified with propaganda and lies that linger today.

There were many heroes of Indigenous resistance. Men and women
who you might want to read more about. Jandamarra, a Bunuba man
who used hit and run tactics against settlers in the Kimberley;[16]
Truganini, a Nuenonne woman, who kept her head high through
brutal and deceitful acts against her body and her loved ones, her dying
wish denied: to allow her remains to rest unmolested;[17] Dundalli, a
Dalla man and resistance hero who stood against invasion for around a
decade;[18] Kebisu, a great sea-warrior and leader of the Kalkalgal people
in the Torres Strait;[19] Tarenorerer of the Tomeginne people, who
trained the remnants of her people to use firearms to fight back;[20] and
Yagan, the Noongar warrior who was feared in the south west.[21] They
were just some of the brave Indigenous people who defended land,
culture, their laws and their families in the Frontier Wars.

If you want to find out about these wars, a brilliant introduction is
the Blackfella Films documentary series, *The Australian Wars*,[22]
directed and narrated by Rachel Perkins. The series succinctly covers
significant battles across the length and breadth of Australia, with the
team interviewing experts and revisiting the journals and oral
accounts from the time.

Another important project that has shed light on the nature of this
violence, *Colonial Frontier Massacres in Australia, 1788–1930*,[23] is led
by historian Professor Lyndall Ryan AM from the University of
Newcastle, in consultation with the Wollotuka Institute and the
Australian Institute of Aboriginal and Torres Strait Islander Studies.
It has documented 413 recorded massacres and estimated that more

than 10,000 Indigenous people were murdered. Oral history suggests there were many more.

A remarkable observation that flows from the data collected was that the attacks during the spread of pastoral settlement in Australia did not decrease as the decades passed – they intensified. More massacres occurred from 1860 to 1930 than in the earlier period of 1788 to 1860.

Let that sink in. It means that the slaughtering of Indigenous people intensified around the time of Federation in 1901 – when we became Australia. The massacres became better organised over time and more brutal.

Professor Ryan and the research team worked with *The Guardian* to share their findings. 'The Killing Times' map[24] shows how Australian massacres were not an aberration, scattered around the edges of colonies.

'They [the massacres] weren't an accident. They were designed to get Aboriginal people out of the way, whether it was to "teach them a lesson", or to make them so timid that they were easier to employ,'[25] said Professor Ryan.

As I travelled the country during the Voice to Parliament campaign, speaking with Australians who were moved to work in solidarity with First Nations people, many told me that it was reports such as *The Guardian*'s article 'The Killing Times' that made them aware of the raw brutality of our colonial past. For many, what stuck in their minds were the examples of the horrors that had happened in places where they themselves found beauty and peace. Take the example of the deaths of Indigenous people in the lovely town of Ballina, established in the 1840s, some 20 kilometres south of Byron Bay on the northern shore of the Richmond River. This place was originally home to the Nyangbal people of the Bundjalung nation, who were almost entirely wiped out in the early 1860s when the city fathers distributed poisoned flour to the Nyangbal, who took it to their camp for cooking. Those who refused to eat the new food survived and found nearly 150 adults dead the next morning.[26]

Soon after I had read about this massacre, my mum told me she overheard a man having a conversation with a woman who was telling him that she had enjoyed traditional bush food on her recent holiday. The man, who believed himself to be so knowledgeable about Aboriginal people, said, 'Well, they have it much easier now. White people gave them flour so they don't need to hunt.'

Along with the massacres of the Frontier Wars, First Nations people were killed through neglect, ongoing cruelty and introduced diseases. I hear from time to time that diseases were responsible for the catastrophic decline in the Indigenous population. Sure, the epidemics were devastating, but I feel Australia's collective responsibility is too easily absolved by blaming tiny microbes and the like. After all, from the turn of the eighteenth century, the British had used inoculations to contain smallpox in the North American colonies. They knew what the impact of smallpox would be. But they let Indigenous people die. The same can be said about the untreated tuberculosis and syphilis that decimated populations in Tasmania and Victoria.

ooooo

There were always people who were prepared to listen and then speak out against the massacres: stockmen who were first-hand witnesses and told the truth about what 'dispersal' actually meant, journalists who published their stories, missionaries who tried to intervene and protect Indigenous people, lawyers who sought some kind of justice. With First Nations witnesses, they tried to have the stories heard but very few wanted to listen. It was so much easier to pretend that the original owners of this country had just gone away.

Today, 'The Killing Times' map and all the shocking but invaluable research by Professor Lyndall Ryan and her team, as well as works by writers and historians such as Professor Marcia Langton, Professor John Maynard and David Marr, show us that massacres took place around the country. Terrible numbers of Indigenous lives were lost, and thousands fought bravely in their attempts to protect their families, their land and their cultures.

Among the many massacres that killed our people, perhaps the best known today is the one that took place at Myall Creek, in northern New South Wales, in 1838. In mid-May 2023, I travelled to the Myall Creek site from Sydney with author and columnist Peter FitzSimons, who was writing for the *Sydney Morning Herald*'s 'Myall Creek Apology' series.[27] We were joined by Uncle Kelvin Brown, who is a local Indigenous expert, and Peter Stewart, the author of *Demons at Dusk: Massacre at Myall Creek*,[28] which gives a detailed historical account of the legal tussle that followed the massacre.

On that trip, I witnessed the healing power that comes when non-Indigenous people, whether they are the direct descendants of those involved in a massacre or a local concerned with making peace with the past, actively pursue reconciliation. The memorial is also testament to the need for recognition.

When Peter FitzSimons and I had dinner with Uncle Kelvin, Kamilaroi Elder Sue Blacklock and some of her family, we talked about the ongoing prejudice in the New England region. But there are beacons of hope. There was the ANTaR group that organised a packed-out Yes campaign town hall meeting in Armidale. There is an annual commemorative event and the memorial to the Myall Creek story, a story on the journey to justice. Sue and Uncle Kelvin were proud of the memorial, and how it educates thousands of locals and even more who are passing by. I imagine that visitors feel what I felt. Horror, then deep sadness, and then an urge to do more – to go out, stand together, and make sure that such racism never happens again.

While the first massacres started in the 1790s, they continued into the twentieth century. The last to be recorded was at Coniston in the Northern Territory in 1928. Think about that – it was less than 100 years ago.

At the ninetieth anniversary of the Coniston massacre, the Northern Territory Police Commissioner Reece Kershaw apologised for this state-sanctioned killing of Aboriginal people, and Liza Dale-Hallett, the great-niece of Constable George Murray who led the massacre, said, 'We are here again today because we believe that facing our history, Australia's history, is so important to our futures. And these stories are still not being heard.'[29]

CHAPTER 5

Becoming Australia

The forefathers of the Commonwealth of Australia were all white men; they were the authors of our Constitution, without even acknowledging the voices of women or Indigenous peoples. Indigenous people were explicitly written out of it. The colonies, and then the states once they federated, increasingly regarded them as a dying race.

The first Prime Minister, Sir Edmund Barton, who was also a founding justice of the High Court, said in 1898 that it was important that the Constitution provide the Federation with the power to make special laws about any race 'to regulate the affairs of the people of coloured or inferior races who are in the Commonwealth'.[1]

And so it went that the Indigenous people who were not killed in the epidemics and massacres were relegated to the margins of society. The state parliaments made laws and curfews to keep even fair skinned Indigenous people out of white areas and towns. Streets named Boundary Street marked the limits.

The remaining Indigenous populations were herded onto missions and reserves, under the control of a 'protector'. These were haphazard efforts to 'smooth the dying man's pillow'[2] – a semblance of protection – while they died out.

Australia's second Prime Minister, Sir Alfred Deakin, continued the White Australia project. He declared that social Darwinism was running its natural course for the masses of Indigenous victims. In 1901 he claimed that 'In another century, the probability is that Australia will be a White Continent with not a black or even dark skin among its inhabitants.'[3]

Yes, they were slaves

> It has been conclusively proved … that white men cannot and will not do the work done by niggers in the field, and … that if white labour were available, it would only be at wages which the planters could never afford to pay. The sugar industry is entirely dependent upon coloured labour.[4]
> –Harold Finch-Hatton, Plantation owner in Mackay, 1886

My good friends from Gurindji Country in the Northern Territory can attest to the depravations of slavery in Australia. When white people first arrived on their Country in 1879 looking for profitable land, relations were friendly. But the settlers insidious intent was hidden until they returned five years later with their herds of cattle. The Gurindji and Aboriginal people from nearby First Nations were forced into slave labour on cattle stations like Wave Hill.

As the Aboriginal people were reeling from massacres, introduced diseases and dispossession, without the same access to hunting grounds or safe access to water, they were easily bonded to work for meagre rations – some flour, tobacco, sugar, tea and beef bones. At one stage, the Vesteys, who owned Wave Hill Station, became concerned that their Aboriginal labour supply was dwindling. They commissioned two anthropologists, Ronald and Catherine Brendt, to advise on how their workers' fertility could be improved.

The anthropologists found 'atrocious' conditions. Mothers and babies were dying during birth, and they witnessed a Gurindji woman's arrival at hospital carrying a long dead foetus in her womb.[5] Despite the obvious recommendations that conditions should be improved if they wanted to maintain their slave labour, the company resisted.

I write more about the history of the Gurindji and their protest against slavery, the Wave Hill Walk-Off, later in this chapter and I also recommend Charlie Ward's book, *A Handful of Sand*, as an excellent resource.

ooooo

In Australia, the word 'slavery' generally isn't used and many people pretend it never happened here. Other words are used instead, but their meaning is the same. We say 'blackbirding', which was when Aboriginal people and South Sea Islanders were kidnapped and forced to work; 'indentured workers', referring to the contracts that bound them; 'domestics', which were mostly women and children under state 'protection' or 'training', who were forced into service for white masters, and 'working for rations' as has been mentioned earlier.

We haven't really admitted that this nation benefited from Indigenous people's unpaid labour, which continued around the country until late last century. Two recent prime ministers, Tony Abbott[6] and Scott Morrison,[7] have actively denied or downplayed the reality that so many First Nations people worked as slaves.

Consider this: if you are paid in scant food rations or very low wages and you are expected to put in long, arduous hours of work each day; if your movements are controlled by your employer and you have no right to take leave even if you are sick; and if you do not have the energy or the time for recreation or cultural ceremonies, does it not follow that you are a slave?

Now imagine this, too: if the only way you may stay or return to your homeland and family is to work for the person who has stolen your land and beaten you into subjugation; if there are strict penalties if you disobey or absconded from your employer, are you a worker, or are you a slave? These were the terms of employment for many Indigenous people up until as late as the 1970s.

Some Australians are wealthy as a direct benefit of the history of stolen land and enslaved Indigenous people. Yet the attitude of too many is that there is no need for recognition or recompense. 'Reparation' should not be a dirty word; instead, we should expect that Indigenous people would receive the compensation they are entitled to from a civilised Australia – a nation that believes in a 'fair go'.

One of the common reasons given for the inequities between Indigenous and non-Indigenous Australians – and I heard it often during the referendum campaign and I still often hear it today – is that Aboriginal people are lazy, they are bludgers who want 'sit-down money' instead of getting a job. Oh, the irony.

When Aboriginal people became entitled to equal wages with the support of the union movement from 1971, the employers sacked and evicted these people from the land they had stolen for their pastoral stations. The Aboriginal people were forced onto welfare camps or to live on the outskirts of towns in conditions of dire poverty.

In many cases, the Elders loved the work they were doing. But they were discarded like lame beasts instead of being paid a reasonable wage. Indigenous people no longer had land, few white people would employ us on equal wages, our youth were not trained and not wanted in the towns and cities, and so what followed was a dependence on welfare.

White opportunists then brought their toxic business of selling alcohol into Aboriginal communities. They made their fortunes on rivers of grog and clouds of hopelessness because what do people do when they have no property, when they have little self-esteem, and when they are forlorn with bucketloads of trauma?

They drink.

What follows the drink?

Violence and antisocial behaviour.

What follows generations of violence and antisocial behaviour?

More children are taken by the authorities and put into abusive situations, and we get more trauma. The stereotypes against us are strengthened. The racism – even if not blatant – is reinforced. And around we go again. This is more than an issue about racism based on the colour of our skin. Have you heard statements such as this: 'There's those lazy blacks on the grog. They should just get off their arse and get themselves a job.'

In any family or group of people who have lived through this cycle, some will work their way out of poverty. But the fact is, we are all wired differently; often people are so detrimentally affected, they can't overcome the poverty and pain. Not without long-term, well-resourced programs and policies, or in other words, a consistent political act of care from 'the rest of us'.

ooooo

During the 2023 referendum campaign, I toured the Clarence Valley with my good friend Julie Perkins, a Gumbaynggirr woman who works for the Gurehlgam Aboriginal Corporation. We spoke at town hall meetings and with local Indigenous groups across the Clarence

Valley. On our drive between Woolgoolga and Maclean, she took me to see the shack she grew up in with her mother.

Julie told me that her family worked for an Indian man who owned the banana plantation on which they lived. After school each day and on school holidays, Julie and her siblings would work in the plantation with the adults, pulling weeds, packing fruit and other odd jobs. Her mum and her grandmother, Ma Skinner, would also walk many kilometres into the town of Red Rock to clean the houses of white families. Her granddad, Pa Skinner, did 'grubbing' for the landholders and their cattle.

As we drove through the green countryside, Julie fondly talked about her hardworking mum. She told me how vividly she remembers watching her mother returning from the employer's house with a pot of food, usually curry.

Julie said that she did not realise until much later in life that the pot of curry was all they were paid. Her granddad was also paid in rations – some flour and tobacco – for his work on the stations.

She told me that her mum was 'so very subservient – a quiet, shy woman who would do anything the landholders asked'.

'Mum thought we were doing okay with curry and being able to grow some veggies to feed us, and even then, I struggled to understand why we should basically beg for food, washing our clothes in the creek. I think of Mum and our family every day … I wish she'd had an easier life.'

Julie Perkins was a child in the 1970s. Her story, like many others across Australia, shines a light on the truth: Aboriginal and Torres Strait Islander people were slaves with fewer rights than other people of colour – in living memory; within the last 60 years.

The Stolen Generations

The power to remove Indigenous children from their families was made legal through colonial and state acts. For example, the *Aborigines Protection Act 1869 (Vic)*, which gave the governor the power to order the removal of any child from their family to a reformatory or industrial school.[8] The aim of the government policies was to forcibly assimilate Indigenous Australians by institutionalising their lighter skinned children. As AO Neville said, to 'breed out the colour'.[9]

An important inquiry into the separation of Indigenous children from their families produced the *Bringing Them Home: National Inquiry into the Separation of Aboriginal and Torres Strait Islander Children from Their Families* Report in 1997. The report records the firsthand accounts of the victims, widely known as the Stolen Generations. It also lays out the laws and policies that made the misery and destruction possible, and the attitudes of the perpetrators.

The first words in the introduction of the *Bringing Them Home* Report are from a Tasmanian survivor's submission:

So the next thing I remember was that they took us from there and we went to the hospital and I kept asking – because the children were screaming and the little brothers and sisters were just babies of course, and I couldn't move, they were all around me, around my neck and legs, yelling and screaming. I was all upset and I didn't know what to do and I didn't know where we were going. I just thought: well, they're police, they must know what they're doing. I suppose I've got to go with them, they're taking me to see Mum. You know this is what I honestly thought. They kept us in hospital for three days and I kept asking, 'When are we going to see Mum?' And no-one told us at this time. And I think on the third or fourth day they piled

us in the car and I said, 'Where are we going?' And they said,
'We are going to see your mother'. But then we turned left to
go to the airport and I got a bit panicky about where we were
going ... They got hold of me, you know what I mean, and I got
a little baby in my arms and they put us on the plane. And they
still told us we were going to see Mum. So I thought she must
be wherever they're taking us.[10]

–Confidential submission 318, Tasmania: removal from
Cape Barren Island in the 1960s

The person in the above submission was one of eight siblings. Each of
the children was fostered separately.

Removing siblings and placing them on different reserves and
missions, or in different foster homes, was common practice, as was
moving children far from where they came from. This was just one
of the measures used to try to stop the survival of languages and
culture. In some instances, babies were taken before their mother
could hold them and children were told, falsely, that their parents had
abandoned them.

To justify taking the children, it was argued that they were being
protected from injury, abuse and neglect at the hands of their own
parents, families and communities. However, their best place was with
their own people and for their people to be treated with dignity and
respect by the white population who wanted them gone.

In the culture I grew up with as a Torres Strait Islander, which is the
same as Aboriginal culture in this regard, we have a broader kinship
structure than modern Western society. All adults, especially within a
clan, have maternal and paternal responsibilities to care for children.
Our aunties and uncles are mothers and fathers. Our cousins are our
brothers and sisters. Family is not necessarily restricted to bloodlines.

The depth of Indigenous communal obligations is still largely misunderstood today.

There was never a justification for what the Stolen Generations experienced while under the state's 'protection'. In the *Bringing Them Home* Report it is recorded that almost one in ten boys and just over three in ten girls were sexually abused when in foster placements.

> When the girls left the home, they were sent out to service to work in the homes and outlying farms of middle class white people as domestics ... On top of that you were lucky not to be sexually, physically and mentally abused, and all for a lousy sixpence that you didn't get to see anyway. Also, when the girls fell pregnant, their babies were taken from them and adopted out to white families, they never saw them again.[11]
>
> —Confidential submission 617, New South Wales: woman removed at eight years with her three sisters in the 1940s; placed in the Cootamundra Girls' Home

If you know little about the Stolen Generations, I encourage you to read the report. You will hear of the heartbreak, anger and disappointment in the voices of the children and their parents. What I found to be truly unambiguous was the sheer racism at all levels of white society that supported the removal of children from their families, and the lifelong and generational cost.

The Stolen Generations were the subject of the National Apology delivered by Prime Minister Kevin Rudd in 2008. The previous Prime Minister, John Howard, had resisted saying sorry on behalf of the nation, maintaining his stance recently that apologising for another generation is 'meaningless'.[12]

I find it hard to understand how one can think that expressing sorrow, remorse and empathy to the living children who were stolen from their families could be described as 'meaningless'. I grew up with some of the Elders who campaigned long and hard for what they knew would be a moment of unification and healing. Watch the footage – look at their faces – when their campaign culminated in the National Apology.[13]

The argument about it being the previous generations' fault is ludicrous, as if people today have not benefited or suffered from the acts of our forebears; as if we commemorate nothing that previous generations of Australians achieved, or lost, in the past. Imagine defunding the Returned and Services League (RSL) nationwide because only the children of our Australian heroes survive.

When Prime Minister Rudd moved the Apology on 13 February 2008, a strong majority of parliamentarians stood with him, including the Opposition Leader at the time, Brendan Nelson, who was as heartfelt in his support as his political opposite.

There was only one front bench politician who boycotted the Apology. That was Peter Dutton. He didn't attend the chamber, refusing to listen to these words:

> *I move:*
>
> *That today we honour the Indigenous peoples of this land, the oldest continuing cultures in human history.*
>
> *We reflect on their past mistreatment.*
>
> *We reflect in particular on the mistreatment of those who were Stolen Generations – this blemished chapter in our nation's history.*
>
> *The time has now come for the nation to turn a new page in Australia's history by righting the wrongs of the past and so moving forward with confidence to the future.*
>
> *We apologise for the laws and policies of successive Parliaments*

and governments that have inflicted profound grief, suffering and loss on these our fellow Australians.

We apologise especially for the removal of Aboriginal and Torres Strait Islander children from their families, their communities and their country.

For the pain, suffering and hurt of these Stolen Generations, their descendants and for their families left behind, we say sorry.

To the mothers and the fathers, the brothers and the sisters, for the breaking up of families and communities, we say sorry.

And for the indignity and degradation thus inflicted on a proud people and a proud culture, we say sorry.[14]

–The Hon Kevin Rudd,
13 February 2008

Following the speeches, Aunty Lorraine Peeters, a Weilwun and Gamilaroi woman, presented a symbolic gift to the Prime Minister and the Leader of the Opposition. There was not a dry eye in that place when she described the gift, a coolamon that was made with glass instead of wood:

Coolamons have carried our children. The gift is a symbol of the hope we place in the new relationship you wish to forge with our people. A relationship that is fragile yet strong. We have a new covenant between our peoples, that we will do all we can to make sure our children are carried forward, loved and nurtured and able to live a full life.[15]

ooooo

Soon after becoming the Opposition Leader and contender for the Prime Minister's job in 2022, Peter Dutton expressed regret for walking out on the National Apology.[16] Indigenous leaders, including myself, accepted his apology in good grace. We hoped it indicated that he might allow Coalition members of Parliament to support the referendum, even if he would not do so himself.

Wiradjuri woman and Minister for Indigenous Affairs Linda Burney said:

> For some, the apology was something to reject and, of course, we all learn and we all grow. I thank the leader of the opposition for his apology today.
>
> It is a good thing that we grow and we learn, but now we have the chance to do something practical together.[17]

I was heartbroken to read Aunty Lorraine's words almost two decades on, understanding that in 2023, we were presented with an opportunity to strengthen the coolamon that carries our babies – to make brittle modern glass into sturdy wood carved by the hands of our ancestors. But the record will show that Peter Dutton did not learn from his mistakes. Maybe he wasn't taught that saying 'Sorry' is more than a word. Maybe he does not understand that an apology should also be a practical commitment to not cause the same harm again.

> I think the Australian people deserve to know the full details of the implications of this policy including the financial ones […] It would beggar belief that they would be contemplating an apology that could open the government up to serious damages claims without knowing what those claims would be.[18]
>
> –Peter Dutton, speaking as the Shadow Finance Minister in 2008

In the months since the failed Voice referendum, I have spoken with many younger Aboriginal and Torres Strait Islander people who watched the Apology. They told me that where they had felt only pessimism, suddenly that day in 2008, they felt hope.

But in 2023, the number of Indigenous children taken into Out of Home Care – where a child who is deemed to be unable to live with their birth families is taken by the state and put into foster or kinship care – hit a new record. In just one year, 22,328 First Nations children were taken from their parents – 10.5 times more than non-Indigenous children.[19] One can only conclude that Australian governments learned nothing from the *Bringing Them Home* Report, although the evidence is all there – take children away from their kinship structures and their culture, and self-destruction becomes more likely. Today our youth suicide rates are three times as high as non-Indigenous children, worse than they were a decade ago.[20] The Apology was important. But taking action, such as changing attitudes and behaviours, should have followed.

Activism is a responsibility

First Nations people have not meekly accepted our exclusion from the power structures and policy-making processes of postcolonial Australia. We have had a long history of calling for change.

Since Federation, against often powerfully entrenched resistance, our people have built a depth of activism and leadership expertise that has slowly but inexorably dragged the nation through to milestones such as the 1967 referendum, land rights legislation, the *Anti-Discrimination Act 1977*, legislated representative bodies such as ATSIC, the Mabo case, the National Apology to the Stolen Generations, and the Uluru Statement from the Heart.

If you look back through the history of our struggle, our calls for each of these achievements were initially rejected by those in power. You would think that they were moments of failure. But each time, these losses built the case to eventual success.

Our ancestors did not let us go the way of the Tasmanian tiger, as many of the founding fathers of Australia had planned for us. When the white bureaucracy controlled our lives and banned practising culture by threat of capital punishment, we defied them, we adapted or passed on culture in secret, or more than 100 years later, we dusted off the white man's journals and revived our languages to teach our children today.

When you learn about Indigenous people's courageous efforts to achieve recognition and justice throughout the past century, you should reflect on why we fight so hard. Think about how we are told in derogatory ways that our activism on the streets is 'radical' or troublemaking, when in reality, our protests are what you too would do to make your children safe. The worsening statistics are as real as our need to take action.

One of the first Indigenous-led political organisations was the Australian Aboriginal Progressive Association (AAPA). It was founded in 1924 by a fellow wharfie, a Worimi man named Fred Maynard. His grandson, Professor John Maynard, became a historian when he was in his forties, after his father suggested he tell Fred's story. Now retired from the University of Newcastle, he has released a second edition of his book about his grandfather's time, *Fight for Liberty and Freedom*. It was in Maynard's book that I first learnt about a second dispossession.

Professor Maynard wrote about how, at the turn of the nineteenth century, some Indigenous communities had gained access to areas of their land for hunting, farming and food gathering. Indigenous farmers toiled to clear the land. Their crops were highly successful. They had an edge on Country, thanks to their deep knowledge about how to cultivate the land. Bruce Pascoe revealed in his bestselling book, *Dark Emu*, that agriculture was practised by Indigenous people well before colonisation.

However, when Indigenous families thrived, often outdoing white farmers, they became increasingly under threat. The second dispossession became imminent.

Families who had worked their land and built a community from their blood, sweat and tears were physically dragged from their properties, or coerced to leave on threat of their children being taken from them. They found themselves on the road with few belongings, no compensation, and nowhere to go but reserves and missions.

A long opposition to celebrating 26 January

The AAPA was one of many representative bodies established throughout the twentieth century, only to be ignored or intimidated until they disappeared. There was also the Australian Aborigines' League (AAL), the Federal Council for the Advancement of Aborigines and Torres Strait Islanders (FCAATSI), the National Aboriginal Conference (NAC), and the National Aboriginal Consultative Committee (NACC).

In the book Kerry O'Brien co-authored with me in 2023, *The Voice to Parliament Handbook*, Kerry shared the details of the rise and fall, the successes and failures of Indigenous representative bodies – a history that informed Indigenous people of the importance of constitutionally protecting a Voice in 2023.

One of the significant protests of the past was led by Yorta Yorta man William Cooper and the Aboriginal Advancement League. They organised a protest in 1938 on the 150th anniversary of the First Fleet's arrival in Australia on 26 January. The gathering in Sydney was called a National Day of Mourning, countering a celebration of the arrival of the First Fleet nearby. At the Day of Mourning, they paid respect to their lost loved ones, and determined a path for recognition and representation.

Indigenous peoples have mourned the invasion of our continent for many more years than 26 January has officially been an Australia Day celebration. The date has varied over the years, but the effects of what it marks has been consistent.[22]

While I understand that Australians would want to celebrate the nation's achievements and identity, what is hard to fathom is why it should be done on 26 January without acknowledging what the date of the invasion means to most First Peoples.

As a Darwin wharfie, I annually mourn the death of wharfies and seafarers whom I had never met. They were killed in World War II when Japanese fighters descended on our small town, sinking ships and destroying the docks where I worked. We mourn those lost during that invasion. We don't celebrate the pilots who came across the seas with ill-intent, we don't call them explorers and pioneers. We mourn in solidarity with all who defended our shores, and most of all, we celebrate peace. I wish I could be allowed this same day of mourning for my own people on 26 January.

Protests, strikes and promises

Each of the early Indigenous organisations I mentioned campaigned for changes to the Constitution because they wanted peace for their people. They called for the federal government to take on responsibility for Indigenous Affairs, rather than the states, which were particularly cruel with their 'Protection' acts. These Indigenous organisations also demanded that First Nations people be counted with full citizenship rights.

Protests such as the Torres Strait Islander Maritime Strike in 1936, the Cummeragunja Walk-Off in 1939, the Pilbara Strike in 1946, the Yolŋu people's Yirrkala Bark Petitions in 1963, and the Freedom Rides led by the great Aboriginal activist, Charlie Perkins AO, were just some of the actions that helped build the public case for the 1967 referendum.

My Gurindji friends also made a great impact. In 1966, their leader, Vincent Lingiari, and 200 Aboriginal stock workers and domestics went on strike, starting their long walk toward freedom.[23] Early in the morning on 23 August, they set off from Wave Hill Station with the sun at their backs. They carried their babies and meagre belongings, staying off the roads to avoid angry white men. The Elders remembered the bloodshed from massacres only decades before, making their protest even more courageous.

The Gurindji people were still on strike in 1967 when the referendum was held. It remains the most successful referendum in Australian history. It asked voters to consider this question:

'Do you approve the proposed law for the alteration of the Constitution entitled "An Act to alter the Constitution so as to omit certain words relating to the people of the Aboriginal race in any state and so that Aboriginals are to be counted in reckoning the population"?'[24]

The positive outcome provided the Federal Parliament with the power to set the Indigenous policy agenda and to count all Indigenous people in the national census.

The Gurindji people's strike continued for eight long years, in the face of intimidation from the government and cattle industry. They rallied popular support with the help of unions and university students. They established a community in a place of their choosing, a place that they called Daguragu, as it had been known for thousands of years.

For years, the Australian Government denied protesting Aboriginal people any rights to the lands that were stolen from them. The Gurindji Walk-Off was one of many actions nationwide at the time; another was the Aboriginal Tent Embassy, established on the lawns in front of the old Parliament House on 26 January 1972. Ironically, the protesters in Canberra were labelled as 'trespassers'.[25]

Their fortunes changed when Gough Whitlam became Prime Minister in 1972. In an election campaign speech he had declared: 'We will legislate to give Aborigines [sic] land rights – not just because their case is beyond argument, but because all of us as Australians are diminished while the Aborigines are denied their rightful place in this nation.'[26]

In 1975, Whitlam travelled to Daguragu, where he met Vincent Lingiari. In a ceremony, captured in an iconic photo,[27] Whitlam poured a handful of sand into the Gurindji leader's, a moving gesture symbolic of handing back land.

For almost a decade now, I have participated in the annual festival the Gurindji organise to celebrate the anniversary of the Walk-Off. I take part in it as a leader of the union that lent the Gurindji people a helping hand during the years of the Walk-Off. Freedom Day is the name of the festival. It is also the name of a children's book I wrote with Lingiari's granddaughter, Rosie Smiler, *Freedom Day: Vincent Lingiari and the story of the Wave Hill Walk-Off*.

The Whitlam government was a breath of fresh air for Aboriginal and Torres Strait Islander people. They began the process towards broader land rights, Aboriginal land councils were established, and money began to flow into Indigenous health, housing, legal aid, education and employment. But Gough Whitlam's time in leadership didn't last long. The same man who had represented the cattle barons against claims for equal wages in the 1960s, Sir John Kerr, had become Governor General. He sacked Whitlam in 1975.

Whitlam's successor, Prime Minister Malcolm Fraser, did see some of Whitlam's visionary policies through. He legislated Northern Territory land rights and established the National Aboriginal Conference (NAC), a thirty-five member representative voice, but Prime Minister Bob Hawke abolished it in 1986.

In 1988, Hawke travelled to a small Aboriginal community called Barunga near Katherine in the Northern Territory. The Aboriginal leaders who had invited him there presented Hawke with the Barunga Statement, calling for a national treaty and for the re-establishment of a national Aboriginal and Torres Strait Islander representative body. He promised to deliver on both.

Hawke dishonoured the promise of a treaty. He was influenced by the Western Australian Premier and National President of the Labor Party, Brian Burke, and by the mining lobby. However, he did deliver on the representative body. The Aboriginal and Torres Strait Islander Commission (ATSIC) was formed in 1990.

A legislated Voice – the Aboriginal and Torres Strait Islander Commission (ATSIC)

ATSIC is an important part of Indigenous and Australian political history. It gave Indigenous people the opportunity to elect Indigenous representatives. The council they formed was granted the power to determine policies and programs that would advance their people. It was still answerable to the federal Minister for Aboriginal Affairs, and subject to the whims of the Parliament in regard to budget and the legislation frameworks they worked in, but it was a truly national and genuinely representative voice. It was the greatest level of interconnected national, regional and local self-determination that we have had to this day.

Representatives were elected every three years by grassroots

Indigenous people, based on thirty-five regional councils that covered the entirety of the nation. The Torres Strait Islands were included in one of sixteen zones, and from the zones, a national board of commissioners was selected, with the Chair initially chosen by the minister.

ATSIC achieved many great improvements for First Nations people. It developed and delivered policies and programs with greater success than ever before. It also created a sense of pride. When I was a teenager, I saw the elections, with local candidates – familiar faces in my community – vying for the opportunity to make a difference. Anything was possible.

From ATSIC came better housing in communities and homework centres that I often used to help me get through years 11 and 12. And while I quickly got a job as a trainee at the Darwin Port when I graduated, my cousins who struggled more than I did went into Indigenous training and employment programs supported by ATSIC, rather than going on the dole.

Human traits such as our egos can get in the way of good governance in any organisation, including ATSIC. It experienced internal political turmoil – we had our own Bad Actors. It should have been up to 'the rest of us', in this case Aboriginal and Torres Strait Islander people, to deal with ATSIC's problems, not the Howard government, which eventually destroyed it.

Mabo and Native Title, Howard and bucketloads of extinguishment

One of the greats in the furthering of Aboriginal and Torres Strait Islander rights in this period was Koiki (Eddie) Mabo. From 1982, he took on the Queensland Government, and then the very legitimacy of the foundations of the nation, in a court case that would establish recognition of Native Title to land in the common law.

Mabo was a fellow Torres Strait Islander from the island of Mer. He worked as a pearler and a cane cutter. When he worked as a railway fettler, he was a union leader and became involved with the local Trades and Labour Council. As a gardener at James Cook University, he met lawyers and academics and his conversations with them sparked ideas in his brilliant mind.

Remarkably, Mabo could quickly grasp Western law, thinking outside the box despite not having a high level of Western education. Importantly, he also knew his customary laws back on his island home.

In the Torres Strait Islands, as an example, an overarching law that was breached by the colonisers with the very first planting of the British flag was 'Tag mauki mauki, Teter mauki mauki': 'Your hands and your feet must not take you to steal what is other peoples.' This Meriam law was part of the evidence submitted when Mabo, with Celuia Mapo Salee, James Rice, Sam Passi and Father Dave Passi, took the government to the High Court to prove that his people had pre-existing title over the land in the case *Mabo v Queensland (No 2)*.

Mabo and his family were subject to threats and racial abuse throughout the ten-year legal campaign, but they would not be intimidated.

On 3 June 1993, the ruling came down from the High Court in favour of Uncle Koiki Mabo. His case overturned the doctrine of *Terra Nullius* – the claim that the Australian continent belonged to no one. The case also established that traditional Indigenous laws, such as Native Title, can coexist with Australian law.

Sadly, Uncle Koiki Mabo wasn't able to celebrate his landmark success with his people. He passed on 21 January 1992, a year before the court made its decision.

In 1991, Paul Keating replaced Hawke as Prime Minister. The following year, soon after the Mabo case put some power back into Indigenous hands, he began to negotiate Native Title legislation with Lowitja O'Donoghue, who was Chair of ATSIC, and a group of dynamic Indigenous leaders.

In December 1992, Keating paved the way for an outcome, speaking the truth about the basis for justice at a speech to the Indigenous community in Redfern, Sydney. His words echoed across the entire nation. No other Australian Prime Minister had been so honest about our collective past.

> … the starting point might be to recognise that the problem starts with us non-Aboriginal Australians. It begins, I think, with that of recognition. Recognition that it was we who did the dispossessing. We took the traditional lands and smashed the traditional way of life. We brought the diseases. The alcohol. We committed the murders. We took the children from their mothers. We practised discrimination and exclusion.
>
> It was our ignorance and our prejudice. And our failure to imagine these things being done to us.[28]

Keating's political interventions were important in the face of vehement opposition to Native Title, especially from state governments, pastoralists and the mining industry, which were deploying the same scare tactics as Dutton did against the National Apology, and as the No campaign did in 2023 to stop Indigenous people from having a Voice.

An agreement was reached between the Keating government and the Indigenous negotiators, ushering in the *Native Title Act 1993*. The new legislation established a process for Traditional Owners to gain

Native Title determinations. It also included a Social Justice Package to advance reconciliation.

In 1995, after wide consultations with their people, ATSIC delivered specific proposals for the social justice package.[29] The proposals included constitutional recognition.

ooooo

An age of improvement in Indigenous affairs came to an end with the election of Prime Minister John Howard in 1996.

When the Wik people in Cape York Peninsula successfully argued in the High Court that pastoral leases did not extinguish their Native Title rights, the Bad Actors began to warn Australians that they might lose their backyards. Howard went so far as to hold up a map of Australia on television, implying that a large portion of Australians might lose their land.[30]

The truth was that no one's property was at risk. Freehold land absolutely extinguished Native Title. The court had only ruled that Native Title and a pastoral lease could co-exist, and the lease holder's rights would prevail in the case of any conflict.

The fear campaign was ultimately successful. After the longest debate in the history of the senate, amendments to the Native Title legislation were passed. Howard had diminished Indigenous people's rights, while simultaneously stoking racism and fear against them.

Prime Minister John Howard was also responsible for the destruction of ATSIC in 2005.

It is worth remembering that as Opposition Leader he had vehemently opposed Hawke establishing the national Indigenous representative body in 1989, claiming that by creating it, the government would 'divide Australian against Australian [creating] a black nation within the Australian nation'.[31]

As explained earlier in this chapter, ATSIC made many great inroads to improve conditions in communities and raise the self-esteem of many Indigenous people. Yes, ATSIC had its problems – a couple of scandalous, unscrupulous types were elected – but democracies will do that from time to time. There is always reform and the law book to throw at criminals.

But the Howard government did not want solutions, they wanted the Indigenous voices to be silenced. They systematically used the media and their privileges in Parliament to amplify ATSIC's problems, softening up the public to the point that when they had the support of the Latham Labor Opposition, the end quickly followed. Decades later, the Minister for Indigenous Affairs at the time, Amanda Vanstone, said that dismantling ATSIC was probably a 'mistake'.[32]

The effectiveness of Howard's campaign to vilify ATSIC was remarkable. When I toured the Great Southern region in 2023 with former Fraser government minister Fred Chaney, holding town hall-style gatherings in Albany and Katanning for the Yes campaign, we found that people held on to Howard's negative rhetoric about the previous representative body.

The Northern Territory Intervention – a racist act

Not long before the 2007 federal election, the Howard government brought in the Northern Territory Emergency Response (NTER), otherwise known as The Intervention.

The policy was framed as a response to the *Little Children are Sacred* Report into sexual abuse of Aboriginal children. The report supported what experts and Indigenous community leaders had been saying for many years: the path to addressing violence in communities and the key to protecting children is to deliver the services that were seriously lacking, and to tackle poverty, unemployment and crowded housing. It specifically recommended partnership with Aboriginal people in the design and implementation of the response.

But the Howard government did the opposite and there were no ATSIC voices to stop him. The Parliament rushed the NTER legislation through with little to no input or consent from the communities that were targeted. Almost overnight, the government gained the power to forcibly lease Aboriginal land and to quarantine welfare. Droves of law enforcement officers, health workers and bureaucrats stampeded into remote Aboriginal communities, stomping on their pride.

John Daley, from the small Aboriginal community of Nauiyu, was the Northern Land Council's Chair in 2007. He told the ABC's Felicity James, 'I think it was done in a way that was so hurtful … When you look at the intervention, it was based on a report – this wasn't the response [the authors] wanted from their report … Why basically ride in there and take away the rights of every traditional owner and Aboriginal person?'[33]

The Intervention was so obviously discriminatory toward Aboriginal people that it required the suspension of the *Racial Discrimination Act 1975* (Cth).[34] It was so extreme, it involved the deployment of the Australian Army to Aboriginal communities, ostensibly in a logistical and administrative role – but can you imagine how the people in these tiny communities felt?

Initially, The Intervention was a $587 million dollar package,[35] and it had a $1.4 billion dollar budget between 2007 and 2012.[36] Many of the changes to legislation were not aimed at addressing child abuse, but conveniently undermined Traditional Owners' land rights.

For the millions of dollars of taxpayer money spent on it, The

Intervention did not save lives, but it cost all Australians in terms of how it widened the gap.

In 2010, the Australian Indigenous Doctors' Association assessed the impact of The Intervention, finding that 'the Intervention could lead to profound long-term damage, with any possible benefits to physical health largely outweighed by negative impacts on psychological health, social health and well-being, and cultural integrity'.[37]

It would be hard to imagine a similarly punitive act against a predominantly non-Indigenous community because of social ills. Regions with high levels of poverty, unemployment and homelessness may have high rates of child abuse and domestic violence, but only Aboriginal communities have had the Australian Army rolled in, their local government disbanded, and the national spotlight shone on each and every one of them, as if they were all guilty of the worst crimes.

The Intervention was passed with the support of the Labor Opposition in 2007 and despite the negative results, aspects of it were continued by Rudd and then Gillard until 2022. Follow the politics of Indigenous Affairs and it seems the welfare of Indigenous children is a favoured wedge the Coalition uses, more recently calling for a royal commission into Aboriginal child abuse.[38]

The Intervention and the politics that accompanied it continue to affect one of the most important relationships in the development of a child. Indigenous fathers, not just in the Territory but nationwide, have felt suspicious eyes on us when we pick up our babies in public. The age-old stereotype was strengthened: beware of Indigenous men, even their children need to be protected from them.

During the Voice referendum, some conservative commentators attacked any suggestion that Australia might have a problem with racism. These were damaging attacks. Of course, average Australians

– soft Yes or soft No voters – were turned off when they thought that those leading the advocacy for a Voice were suggesting that they were racist. No one has ever suggested that all Australians are racist, as the sensationalist headlines purported. I certainly do not. But reread this chapter if you need to. Look at how we became Australia – the Black bodies piled up around Federation. The slavery. The ignorance. The resistance to treating us like equals.

Leaners and lifters

This chapter brings us into more recent times. No less harrowing though, for Indigenous Australians, many of whom felt utterly devastated after so many years of The Intervention policies.

Let's start in 2013. The Rudd and then the Gillard government had kept The Intervention going, but under a new name: Stronger Futures. We also had a new Prime Minister, Tony Abbott, who'd brought a wrecking ball with him.

Before being elected, Abbott declared that he would be 'not just a Prime Minister, but a Prime Minister for Aboriginal Affairs. The first I imagine we have had'.[1] This was as ill-fitting as his self-appointed role as Minister for Women, which he took on once in government.

Behind the façade: unemployment and economic exclusion

Australia, under Prime Minister Abbott and his Treasurer Joe Hockey, was rhetorically divided into 'lifters' and 'leaners'. Lifters were people who worked and paid tax, and leaners were people who weren't rolling in wealth, and who had any reliance on what taxes paid for. Hockey said, 'We must always remember that when one person receives an entitlement from the government, it comes out of the pocket of another Australian.'[2]

The Abbott government's first budget was full of broken promises, taking the axe to education, health and the public broadcasters. But one matter Abbott reneged on that received very little attention was his promise to continue to fund Closing the Gap policies without change. Instead, he slashed $534 million from Indigenous programs and services.

The federal government cuts included $160 million from Indigenous health programs,[3] even though the life expectancy of an Indigenous person was around eight years less overall, and thirteen years less in the Northern Territory.[4] They cut $42 million from Indigenous legal services, even as we were twelve times more likely to go to jail. And $9.5 million was cut from language support, important to our culture, justice, health, education, and more.

In addition to the cuts, Abbott ushered in a new regime of paternalism. His government mashed 150 Indigenous-specific initiatives and services, which were run through the relevant departments such as Housing, Education and Health, into just five programs, all administered by one department: the Department of Prime Minister and Cabinet.[5]

Suddenly, a single department, with little to no expertise in delivering services and programs in remote Aboriginal communities, became responsible for 2000 staff and over 3000 contracts.

The changes to how money earmarked to address Indigenous disadvantage would be spent was called the Indigenous Advancement Strategy (IAS), and the final say on expenditure was with the Minister for Indigenous Affairs. Under Abbott, the Minister was

Senator Nigel Scullion. The strategy was meant to 'improve the way the government did business with Aboriginal communities and improve outcomes',[6] though in effect, it culled programs that were making headway, while favouring applications that were low ranked by Indigenous communities. Scullion came under fire in 2018 because he granted almost half a million dollars of IAS money to non-Indigenous fishing and cattlemen's groups, who were opposing land rights claims.[7]

The Australian National Audit Office slammed the new Indigenous Affairs expenditure scheme, saying it was rushed and administered in opaque ways that 'fell short of the standard required to effectively manage a billion dollars of Commonwealth resources'.[8]

One of the successful programs that the Abbott government destroyed was the Community Development Employment Projects, or CDEP.

First implemented in 1977, CDEP were managed by community-based organisations and local councils. Local people had agency to determine how they would improve community infrastructure, such as building houses, and what services were needed, such as childcare and after-school care. They would receive grants to employ community members part-time who would otherwise be receiving unemployment benefits.

CDEP also helped Indigenous community organisations to establish small enterprises, including commercial cardboard recycling and lawn-mowing.[9] As an example, on the New South Wales south coast, a firewood scheme was supplying wood to both Indigenous and non-Indigenous residents. By 2004, there were 35,000 Indigenous people participating in the program, within 265 local Indigenous organisations.[10]

In many of the places that I have visited across the country, people have told me about the pride they had in what they achieved under CDEP. They said the work they had through these projects felt meaningful because they were doing activities that improved their lives. The projects also brought in capital and equipment that created more opportunities for local self-reliance and self-determination. Importantly, CDEP often had the added benefit of optional additional hours of work to top up wages.

CDEP was replaced in 2015 by what the Abbott government called the Community Development Program (CDP) – a 'work-for-the-dole' program.

Where previously there was a nuanced effort by local managers to give participants meaningful work, control was now handed to work-for-the-dole providers based in cities and major regional centres, often far away from Indigenous communities and their needs. Indigenous organisations, advocacy groups and the Australian Council of Trade Unions (ACTU) quickly condemned the CDP as racist.[11] The new policy was arduous to execute and harmfully punitive.

The difference was stark between the way unemployed Indigenous people were treated under CDP and the way other unemployed Australians were treated under the government's mainstream Jobactive work-for-the-dole program. For example, in the Australian Government's Jobactive program, people on welfare were required to participate for twenty-six weeks each year, and for fifteen hours per week. CDP was for forty-six weeks of the year, for twenty-five hours per week, strictly five hours per day Monday to Friday. Also, the scheme was set up in a way that incentivised providers to sanction participants and to keep them on the program.

Analysis by ANU researcher Lisa Fowkes, carried out sixteen months after the program was implemented, found that the new CDP program was far more effective at penalising participants for breaching its draconian attendance requirements than in engaging them in work for the dole.[12] The Australia Institute quantified this, saying that compared to the mainstream Jobactive program, CDP participants were twenty-five times more likely to receive a standard penalty (no payments for up to eight weeks), and fifty-five times more likely to receive a serious penalty (no payment for eight weeks or more).[13]

That was eight weeks without a cent of income. And it didn't matter if the reason for non-compliance was beyond an individual's control.

What harm do you think is done to a child, a family, a community, a town such as Alice Springs, when a reasonably well functioning employment initiative is suddenly changed dramatically, services cut, and people can't even get the miserable dole? Parents, for example, finding themselves with no money for food or fuel, their child's wants and needs, nothing for eight long weeks.

I will tell you what it does. Across the decade after the start of The Intervention, suicide rates increased by 49 per cent. For Indigenous women, the rate of hospitalisation due to self-harm rose by 120 per cent.[14] And it reasonably follows that the rise in youth crime would also have links to The Intervention and Abbott's wrecking ball.

The result is that Aboriginal people are blamed for these problems.

ooooo

What we can't do is endlessly subsidise lifestyle choices if those lifestyle choices are not conducive to the kind of full participation in Australian society that everyone should have.[15]

–Tony Abbott

Abbott's expectation that Aboriginal and Torres Strait Islander people should move to where there are employment opportunities might make sense if one ignores the history of our people since the invasion, which we have touched on already in this book.

Aboriginal and Torres Strait Islander people will never lose the spiritual and physical ties we have to the lands of our ancestors, no matter what policy a government might try. It is time for a different approach and attitude.

To the greatest extent possible, Indigenous Australians should be supported to live on their traditional lands if they choose to by reconsidering what we class as work. Traditional Owners who put their time and energy into maintaining Indigenous languages, knowledge and culture, and who are teaching the next generations to do the same, are performing a public service. They should be paid at a level that values their efforts and cultural expertise as educators and guardians. These fundamental manifestations of such a rich culture and civilisation are at the heart of this nation's history and vital to its future.

The Indigenous Rangers on Country are a notable example.[16] Indigenous Rangers are Traditional Owners who are employed to look after the environment and all that depends on it. They use traditional knowledge and cultural practices, combined with Western science, and they assist authorities such as Quarantine, Customs, National Parks and Defence. The positive social impacts these programs have are enormous. Not only is being an Indigenous Ranger meaningful work, but they also engage with kids who may be inspired to pursue careers in marine biology, zoology and geology. In my opinion, Indigenous Rangers are as important as any other service that Australians expect our governments to fund, and our investment in them and their continuity should be unquestionably secure.

This way of thinking should not be limited to remote areas where traditional knowledges are still largely intact. We should also value Aboriginal and Torres Strait Islander people who are revitalising damaged strands of culture in other parts of Australia where colonisation was most destructive. Their forms of art and culture may be somewhat evolved, melded into a modern form, made whole through instinct as much as handed-down knowledge, but they are of just as much value to our local, regional and national identities – important to our social cohesion and sense of pride – as are the more traditional ways.

Finally on the matter of lifting our communities from poverty, it is important to note that Traditional Owners remain economically bound by governments and the overpowering influence of wealthy non-Indigenous private interests in their land. As Yawuru man and Vice President (First Nations) at the Australian National University, Professor Peter Yu AM, has been arguing, unless there is the 'development of an economic self-determination framework, Indigenous Australians will continue to be second-class citizens in their own country'.[17]

Indigenous groups are capable of building local economies, establishing independent financial institutions, and generating wealth from their genetic and intellectual property. An excellent example is the Aboriginal Sea Company (ASC) established by Sea Country Traditional Owners in the Northern Territory through the Anindilyakwa, Tiwi, and Northern Land Councils. Since 2022, the ASC has worked with government and non-Indigenous stakeholders to improve legislation and establish a ten-year plan to unlock Traditional Owners' fishing potential. One of their initiatives was the purchase of ten of the Northern Territory's mud crab fishing licences, helping Indigenous Sea Country Traditional Owners to become the single largest licence holder. The licences have been leased back to an experienced industry operator who will train local Aboriginal people to do commercial fishing and eventually take over the business.

The initiatives that work, such as this one, tend to be instigated by local Aboriginal and Torres Strait Islander people and communities, not governments or non-Indigenous corporations. The late former Northern Land Council Chairman, Dr Bush-Blanasi, said of the ASC and First Nations empowerment on their lands: 'Aboriginal people have fought hard for rights to land and sea country and the Northern Land Council has taken up the fight for almost 50 years. We have had many critics of land rights over the years, but the sky hasn't fallen in. It's good for the economy and it's good for Traditional Owners. Everyone benefits.'[18]

An invitation to listen

In 2015, Aboriginal and Torres Strait Islander leaders called for a crisis meeting with Prime Minister Tony Abbott and Opposition Leader Bill Shorten.

From the meeting came the Kirribilli Statement. Signed by the thirty-nine Indigenous leaders who attended, the Statement confirmed Indigenous support for constitutional recognition in a way that lays 'the foundation for the fair treatment of Aboriginal and Torres Strait Islander peoples into the future'.[19]

To avoid the process stalling, the leaders proposed that a Referendum Council be established with the resources required to organise 'an ongoing dialogue between Aboriginal and Torres Strait Islander people and the parliament, based on the significant work already completed, to negotiate on the content of the question to be put to referendum'.[20]

Abbott agreed, though he was soon replaced by a new Prime Minister, Malcolm Turnbull. The Turnbull government established the Referendum Council that the Indigenous leaders had proposed.

The Council was made up of equal numbers of non-Indigenous and

Indigenous persons. It went about the task of bringing Aboriginal and Torres Strait Islander people together, region by region, in dialogues about what form of constitutional recognition they would support. Once the dialogues agreed on their favoured reform, the final task of each dialogue was to elect delegates from the region to go to a culminating convention in the heart of the nation – the Uluṟu National Constitutional Convention.

The Convention was held between 23 and 26 May 2017. I was a delegate elected from the region around Darwin. I won't go into great detail here about the Convention as I have written about my experiences while sharing the insights of others in my book *Finding the Heart of the Nation: The journey of the Uluṟu Statement towards Voice, Treaty and Truth.*

The historical significance of the Convention was the consensus we reached on the final morning. We were more than 250 delegates from across the continent, and together we endorsed the Uluṟu Statement from the Heart. The Uluṟu Statement proposed the favoured reforms in the regional dialogues in sequence. First, a constitutionally enshrined Voice to Parliament, and second, a Makarrata Commission to supervise a process of agreement making between governments and First Nations, and truth-telling about our history.

Soon after the Uluṟu Statement was announced, a poll indicated that around 49 per cent of Australians might vote Yes at a Voice to Parliament referendum. But sadly, Prime Minister Turnbull was not supportive. He dismissed the proposal for a Voice in October that year.

Mountains more work was then done by Indigenous advocates to build public and political support for a referendum. There was no public funding for that work. My six years of advocacy were largely supported by the Maritime Union of Australia, in line with the policy our members had determined at our Quadrennial National Conference.

When the Labor government was elected in May 2022, Anthony Albanese declared in his victory speech, 'On behalf of the Australian Labor Party, I commit to the Uluru Statement from the Heart in full.'[21] I literally danced with joy.

Around the nation that election night, Aboriginal and Torres Strait Islander people were dancing with me. We were hopeful. We had worked hard to convince both the Coalition and Labor to take a referendum to the people. With my Labor Party connections through the union movement, it was my responsibility to help bring the left onside. In 2018, support for the Uluru Statement from the Heart became Labor national policy. In 2022 it was an election promise. When Prime Minister Albanese won power, the polls indicated that public support was up to 60 per cent in favour of the referendum. The stars were aligning.

After their election, Prime Minister Albanese, the Minister for Indigenous Affairs, Linda Burney, and the Special Envoy for the implementation of the Uluru Statement, Senator Patrick Dodson, quickly assembled a Referendum Working Group to guide the government on the timing and wording for a Voice referendum. I was one of twenty members, chosen for our experience, expertise and commitment to the cause.

Our group was supported by a panel of legal experts. Its members included some of the most respected law practitioners and academics in the country, such as former Chief High Court Judge Robert French, Former High Court Justice Kenneth Hayne, Indigenous experts Professor Megan Davis and Professor Asmi Wood, and academics, Professors Anne Twomey and George Williams.

Indigenous leaders, constitutional experts and the government, together, negotiated the words for the referendum in good faith. After months of discussions, on 23 March 2023 we announced the words for the proposed constitutional amendment. The wording was supported by constitutional experts, law councils around the country, and the Commonwealth Solicitor General as safe and true to the intent: that henceforth, if the answer was Yes, the First Peoples would be recognised, and they may have a say about the decisions being made about them – nothing more, and nothing less.

A proud movement for recognition

I met some wonderful Australians in the five years of campaigning for the recognition of the Uluṟu Statement until Albanese was elected in 2022, and then during the 2022–23 campaign for the referendum. Big-hearted people who were from reconciliation groups, unions, religious groups, ethnic societies and the remotest of Indigenous communities. Some were mums and dads whose child brought a copy of the Uluṟu Statement home from school because their teacher recognised the importance of their students learning about Aboriginal and Torres Strait Islander history and culture. Some were grandparents and even great-grandparents who decorated their retirement homes with Yes merchandise.

In the months it took to determine the details of the referendum, the Board of Australians for Indigenous Constitutional Recognition established the Yes23 Campaign, raising funds, employing staff and signing up volunteers. We had a Board from across the political spectrum, co-chaired by Rachel Perkins and prominent non-Indigenous solicitor Danny Gilbert AM, with campaign director, Quandamooka man Dean Parkin. As Parkin established his team, Yes groups quickly formed, popping up in almost every town and city.

Former Liberal MP and ultra-marathon runner Pat Farmer AM was on the road before the campaign proper started, in an epic run around Australia. He called the effort, 'Run for the Voice'. The

61-year-old set out from Hobart on 23 April 2023. He reached Uluru on 11 October 2023, three days before the referendum, after running every day. He covered more than 14,000 kilometres.

As Farmer made his way down the east coast, I ran with him for a few kilometres in Bundaberg, Queensland, and again in Newcastle, New South Wales. He set a good pace to reach his goal before 14 October, taking every opportunity to engage with the public, encouraging them to vote Yes. Sadly, his ultimate goal – constitutional recognition for First Nations people – was denied.

There were many acts of sacrifice and courage on the Yes side. Torres Strait Islander woman Tanya Hosch is a great example. In her home city of Adelaide on 31 August, at the launch of the Yes campaign when the Prime Minister announced the referendum would be held on 14 October, Hosch delivered a speech in a venue on the outskirts of Adelaide, rallying supporters only two weeks after she'd had a leg amputation. Tanya Hosch bravely stood on one leg, only the day after leaving the hospital, to give an example of how the health system lets Indigenous people down. The Voice, she argued, would address such policy failures.

Another inspirational Indigenous figure was Michael Long. The Tiwi Islander AFL star had defied racism in the sport in the 1990s. In 2004, frustrated at the plight of his people, he decided to take action, walking from his home in Melbourne to Parliament House in Canberra. He took the initiative again in the lead-up to the referendum, replicating the walk to bring attention to his hope that Australia would say, 'Yes.'

Both the Elders and a new generation of Aboriginal and Torres Strait Islander advocates for First Nations justice stood tall during the campaign. They faced the cameras, staring down the intimidation and sensationalism, giving their all while trying to reach over the ruckus to take Australians by the hand.

One of the great highlights for me was the 'Walk for Yes' marches in every capital city across the weekend of 16–17 September. The marches happened in many smaller towns and Aboriginal communities as well. At the march in Brisbane where I spoke, we expected 8000 supporters, but estimates were as high as 20,000 people, pouring over the bridge between Southbank and the city. The numbers were well beyond expectations at each of the events around the nation.

I wish I had the space in this book to mention the many more wonderful moments I experienced or heard about. Even if I tried, I would always fall short. This is why I want people to write about their experiences.

I want you to record what you witnessed and how you contributed to convincing more than six million Australians to walk with us. Perhaps publish your stories, share them with others, ensure your stories are there for your families generations from now, because throughout the campaign, there was much to be proud of and much that future Australians can learn from.

Share the love and joy you felt, but also the many tough moments too. It was hard work for the generous, selfless and dedicated Yes campaign volunteers. I hope they share how they felt the brunt of the worst aspects of our country – how they were hurt by the effects of the terrible lies and disinformation, the fearmongering, racism and hate that the Bad Actors stirred up against a modest proposition to listen to what Aboriginal and Torres Strait Islander have to say.

Let's take up the pen, the platform – lift our voices – and write, teach and sing the truth into history.

I want to write my deep gratitude into history right here. I hope all you good people who proudly and actively walked with us, or stood tall for your mob, read this and hear your names in my heartfelt words. Thank you. Ultimately, history will validate your actions.

Which brings us to the present.

Since the referendum, we can no longer just hold the white forefathers of this country responsible for the absence of First People's voices in Australia's founding document. It was we who excluded them, in our time, under our watch. If we want peace and justice in our lifetimes, the campaign must continue.

PART 3

What's next?

The final part of this book is about taking action. It is about what you can start to do today. Use your creativity and your own ideas, and also accept that others with the same goal might be doing things differently. With so many demands on everyone's time, you might only be able to take small but powerful actions, such as fitting in an occasional conversation with colleagues about justice for First Nations people or wearing a T-shirt with a slogan that shows your support. These are important and valuable ways to continue the campaign for justice and recognition for our people.

CHAPTER 7

Understanding what we are up against

Following the Voice to Parliament referendum, Aboriginal and Torres Strait Islander people remain as determined as ever to achieve justice. We will continue to advocate for change because it is necessary for the peace and prosperity of our children, our communities and, in turn, for all Australians.

In the future, much will be said about what happened in 2023. There will be in-depth discussions about how the various demographics responded to the Yes and No tactics. Prominent actors will share blow-by-blow accounts about the push and shove during the campaign. Fingers will be pointed and allegations made about who held what back, who would have and could have made a difference, why someone's brilliant ideas would have won the day; if only, if only.

But in this book, we are striving to look forward with purpose. We are taking with us the lessons from the past so we can see justice for First Nations peoples in our lifetimes.

What's next will be better than yesterday if more of us understand the difference between truth and lies. It is also important to understand that as we continue to strive for justice, we are far from being alone.

Australians want progress

Around 60,000 volunteers joined the campaign, many of whom had never taken part in any type of campaign before. Also, six million people voting Yes is a substantial part of the population in Australia.

Before the referendum, Indigenous Australians, who are less than 4 per cent of the population, were working for justice for our people. Now we know that together with our supporters, almost 40 per cent of Australians are striving to achieve this goal.

On the other hand, the No vote was not Australians saying no to Indigenous rights. After all, I believe most No voters want to see a better future for Indigenous children. However, the No campaign's catch cry – 'If you don't know, vote No' – was an effective slogan.

Since the referendum, some Bad Actors have been using the outcome to argue against any recognition of Indigenous Australia at all, claiming that the No vote was a 'clear rejection of the Uluru Statement'.[1] That, in my opinion, is a purposeful misrepresentation of the outcome.

Conservatives in Queensland and Victoria, for example, have announced they will repeal treaty legislation if they are elected. And in some local government areas, councils have removed the traditional Welcome and Acknowledgement of Country from their meetings and events.[2]

It appears to me that there is a greater reluctance to demonstrate leadership and vision in Indigenous affairs since the referendum. While the Albanese government has wasted no time introducing some practical policy advances, such as in Indigenous housing,[3] employment[4] and education,[5] we cannot lose sight of the need for structural and systemic reforms – to address the core of the problem, the torment of our powerlessness.[6]

A 'much unloved people'

In the introduction to this book, I quoted from Noel Pearson's 2022 Boyer Lectures. He described the relationship between Indigenous and non-Indigenous Australians, laying bare the uncomfortable truth that Indigenous Australians are 'a much unloved people'.

You may have thought Pearson was being a little harsh to suggest this. I would have too if I had not personally witnessed the truth behind his words many times in my life.

I learnt just how unfriendly white Australians could be to my people when I was around nine years old. After a wonderful and memorable afternoon at the Darwin Show, my parents, younger sisters and I were driving out of the dusty car park. As we hit the Stuart Highway, a red ute drove alongside us with a group of young white men sitting in the tray. It bewildered and frightened us when, unprovoked, the men spat vile racist abuse at us – 'Filthy abos', 'Dirty boongs', and worse. Then they sped away.

My strongest memory from the bicentenary year, when I was eleven, is another example. Our family was on a long driving holiday, going from Darwin, down the Stuart Highway to Adelaide, and returning home via the east coast. To make the holiday affordable, we would often pull over to cook and eat dinner on the side of the road. Dad would drive through the night, napping in the car if he became too tired, my mum asleep in the front passenger seat and us three kids rugged up in the back. I experienced some of the best of our country on that trip. I also experienced the worst. In a small country town in the south of Queensland, a one-hotel sort of town, the proprietors of the hotel wouldn't serve us. Perhaps we were going to stay in a hotel because Dad was particularly tired that evening. But he drove on. His anger would have kept him awake that night.

Just today, as I write this chapter in January 2024, I have received a text message from an anonymous person who obviously holds strong views about Indigenous Australians. I write it here exactly as it was written.

> if this number is correct it should be thomas mayo . mr mayo , as i live in australia , i know what an australian aboriginals appearance is , and it is not you , david gulpilil yes but not you , i remind you that yes , the fullblood aboriginals were here first , then people from many other nation , then wannabes like you , you and your ilk are a by product of fullbloods and us , so , remember we were here before you (wannabes) . the voice was decided with a NO , you lost , move on

I wouldn't usually share a message like this, though it is one of many. I have received worse: menacing questions about family members and death threats. I felt that sharing this one as an example is important, though, because we need to remove any doubt about how horribly racist some Australians are.

Familiarity matters

During the referendum campaign, it became clear to me that many Australians do not know who Indigenous people are. This unfamiliarity made voters susceptible to the No campaign's scare tactics and methods to confuse voters so they would turn against us.

It is easier for a person to believe a vicious rumour about a stranger than about a friend. Familiarity matters. This plays out in the way many Australians are led to believe terrible lies about Aboriginal and

Torres Strait Islander people, because in the main, they don't know us.

That we are strangers to most Australians makes sense. As I mentioned earlier, Aboriginal and Torres Strait Islander people make up less than 4 per cent of the population, spread across the vastness of one of the largest countries (by land mass) on Earth. But the reason for the negative and unfriendly views goes much deeper, both historically and as part of the Australian psyche today.

In his Boyer Lectures, Noel Pearson mentioned WEH Stanner, a non-Indigenous anthropologist who gave his own Boyer Lectures in 1968. Stanner explained how Australia's sense of its past, its collective memory, had been built on a state of selective forgetfulness that couldn't be 'explained by absent-mindedness'.

To get his point across he used a powerful analogy showing how ignorance toward Indigenous Australians – our existence, our humanity and our rights – has been by design. Stanner said: 'It is a structural matter, a view from a window which has been carefully placed to exclude a whole quadrant of the landscape. What may well have begun as a simple forgetting of other possible views turned under habit and over time into something like a cult of forgetfulness practised on a national scale.'[7]

There are those of us – both Indigenous and non-Indigenous people – who have broken the spell and stepped up to Stanner's window. We have seen a vision of an Australia that includes the perspectives of Aboriginal and Torres Strait Islander people. But we must be aware that the cult of forgetfulness continues, maintained by a few ultra-conservative historians, shock-jock radio commentators, columnists and TV hosts, and it has a real effect on the psyche of many of the people we love.

These immoral influencers have made a career from a niche in the media that exploits how little Australians know about Indigenous people. They exaggerate, misinform and use fallacies to generate clicks, to create fear. They loudly ask questions without accepting the answers – which come from Indigenous leaders and eminent legal authorities – as a way to cause confusion. Most egregiously, they lie when they claim that Indigenous people want Australians' personal property, especially their land.

When people are told to mistrust Aboriginal and Torres Strait Islander people, and when combined with the deep-seated amnesia that Stanner speaks of, it is more likely these people will resist change.

The referendum was an opportunity for voters to face up to the past and present injustices. And many responded positively. There were valuable, open conversations that I and many supporters enjoyed across the country. But the cult of forgetfulness and fearmongering continued its work – the result was that people were angry at us. Such strong feelings were certainly felt at the polling booths.

The greatest challenge in achieving justice for Indigenous Australians is twofold. First, we need to understand the inherent prejudice that will take a strong and united effort to overcome. Secondly, we need to help fair-minded Australians become familiar with the truth of who we First Peoples are.

We must use truth to protect our fellow Australians from the lies they will continue to hear.

A note about Bad Actors

Almost 60 years on from Stanner's groundbreaking lecture, voters were invited to widen their view through that window in order to appreciate the full vista of who we are as Australians. We had an opportunity to dispel the cult of forgetfulness at its core, through constitutional recognition. Collectively, we were on the cusp of stepping toward the window. But some chose to obstruct the view.

What would compel people to stand in the way of such an important revelation? Noel Pearson outlined what proved to be an irresistible temptation for Bad Actors in his Boyer Lectures when he went on to say:

> If success in the forthcoming referendum is predicated on our popularity as a people, then it is doubtful we will succeed. It does not and will not take much to mobilise antipathy against Aboriginal people and to conjure the worst imaginings about us and the recognition we seek. For those who wish to oppose our recognition it will be like shooting fish in a barrel. An inane thing to do – but easy. A heartless thing to do – but easy.[8]

In any analysis of the referendum, whether in a conversation at home or at work, or in an article, book or essay you might read, it may be that you agree with arguments about flaws in the Yes campaign; you may speculate on what the Prime Minister could have done differently; or in hindsight, you might believe we should have waited for more favourable economic times.

While all aspects of the attempted constitutional recognition of the First Peoples is fair game, we should always remind people that the most significant factor that turned Australians from a majority who would vote Yes in the early polls, into a majority who voted No, were the powerful few – the Bad Actors – who chose to use the referendum as a weapon in their ideological wars against peace and justice in our country.

We should also remember that a vast majority of Indigenous communities voted Yes.

CHAPTER 8

Flooding the zone with truth and hope

I t's amazing how vulnerable people can be to a well-crafted and well-disseminated disinformation campaign, yet there are few legal repercussions for dishonesty in politics. Donald Trump in the United States is a case in point: he has shown that consistent lying can overwhelm the truth. The referendum confirmed the method works in Australia too.

It is important to understand that Bad Actors in Australia will continue to use the tactics that Trump's chief strategist, Steve Bannon, bragged about with regard to spreading misinformation on social media: to 'flood the zone with shit'.[1] We can expect a lot more shit to come our way as First Nations people progress treaty talks in Victoria and Queensland, as state governments establish legislated Voices, such as the one in South Australia, and in the lead-up to the next federal election.

How do we counteract these tactics? Part of the answer is to flood the zone with truth and hope.

Building bridges

In the final chapter I will share my thoughts on a formula for change, including a list of things we can do. But the single most important action we can take as individuals is to actively bring truth and hope to anyone and everyone we can.

Spreading hope begins at a personal level. You can share what you have learnt in this book, patiently and respectfully, with your friends and family, your neighbours and workmates, the stranger who seems to have an open mind. Your informed conversations will help shine a light on the truth while dispelling the shadowy disinformation and fake news that are all too prevalent.

Be prepared for encounters with people who believe the lies that have been told about First Nations people. Try not to blame them – we are all susceptible to disinformation. Keep in mind that some of us are vulnerable because we feel overwhelmed and powerless within our own lives. Others hold prejudices that are so deeply entrenched, they believe Indigenous people are inferior.

Van Badham, my good friend from the union movement and the author of *QAnon and On: A short and shocking history of internet conspiracy cults*, told me that those who go down the rabbit hole of conspiracy theories sometimes do so because of the social group with which they surround themselves. This could be an online chat community or a toxic culture amongst friends or at work.

It is important to be aware of the latter group. I have shared with you how real and how nasty racism can be. People who are racist will rarely admit that they are, partly because they may not even know it about themselves. Partly because they will actively search for public commentators in supposedly reputable newspapers and TV channels who will reinforce their views.

You will save time and heartache by learning to avoid wasting your time and energy on someone once they have shown that they will never budge. Especially if the person is offensive, aggressive, or if your senses are calling for caution.

While you will meet people who are hostile to the truth, only a minority will not be moved by your efforts – even if at the very least, you have caused them to think a little more deeply about their own views. Push on. You will find that many Australians are coming from a genuinely good place with minds open to learning the truth.

Without a doubt, as I travelled the nation speaking with thousands of Australians, I found that the most effective way to engage with good people who have misconceptions was to be patient and to listen to them. Find common ground to build rapport, and then acknowledge the source of their fear or concern. Talking down at someone will never change their mind; instead, hear them out, address each point they raise with logic, offer guidance and invite them to find out more.

I could see the effectiveness of this approach in the feedback I received from Yes supporters who regularly worked on information stalls at markets and shopping centres. They reported that initially they experienced hostility and indifference, but they kept turning up, week after week, kindly offering to engage in respectful conversations. As the weeks progressed, some people began to warm to the Yes volunteers because they were familiar. Eventually they engaged in constructive discussions. The volunteers helped some people change their vote from No to Yes.

Patience, persistence, resilience and perseverance do make a difference, all accompanied by respect and a willingness to listen.

When you find that you or the person you are talking to are growing frustrated, don't lose your cool; end the conversation on a positive note if you can, and if possible, revisit the conversation when you both feel calm. Your friends, family and acquaintances are important to you, and clearly, you are to them because they are engaging with you on the topic. Don't ruin your relationships. Take your time.

Engaging in critical thinking is vital

Since the internet and the increasing pervasiveness of social media, and now with Artificial Intelligence in the mix as well, it is harder than ever to determine fact from fiction. This makes critical thinking vital to achieving positive change, not just for the future of Aboriginal and Torres Strait Islander people, but for all Australians.

Critical thinking is the process of deciding what is true or false by using sound logic and by checking for flaws in one's sources of information, without allowing long-held beliefs, emotions or biases to disguise reality.

We should encourage our friends and family to use critical thinking; explain how you question and check what you hear in the media and other sources as a way to find the truth. Perhaps ask if they would like to join you to research and discuss some important issues together.

Help people to understand the media landscape so they can determine what is fact and what is false. I have great trust in news sources such as the Australian Broadcasting Corporation (ABC), the Special Broadcasting Service (SBS), the NITV, the newspapers *National Indigenous Times*, *The Saturday Paper* and *The Guardian*, rather random YouTubers, TikTokers, radio shock jocks and some commentators. It is important to keep in mind that some media outlets use a business model that relies on sensationalism – stoking fear and playing to our worst voyeuristic tendencies – to whip up an audience so they can sell advertising.

Everyone today can be involved in conversations about critical thinking. You may be a teacher who integrates critical thinking into your lessons. You may be a union official or a business leader with an opportunity to roll out critical thinking awareness and education in your organisation. You may make it a kitchen-table subject with family and friends at home.

How to respond to lies and misconceptions with the truth

In the following pages, I address a few statements that I often hear. This information will help you to respond to the lies about Indigenous Australians that lead to the misconceptions you may confront in your conversations in support of justice and recognition. I offer this as a guide; the responses I give here are not definitive, but might be a useful starting point for you in your discussions.

Not all Indigenous people agree with ...

When you hear the argument that something is or isn't supported by Indigenous people, there are a few things you should consider.

The most certain measure of what Indigenous people want was the national poll at the 2023 referendum. We now know that a majority of Indigenous Australians voted Yes to a constitutionally enshrined Voice to Parliament. But, on a day-to-day basis, other than rare and substantially less accurate polls, how does anyone know for sure what most Indigenous people want?

The reality is that, as is the case for any other group of people, not all Aboriginal and Torres Strait Islander people will be in full agreement with each other all of the time. But common sense tells us that if we want to understand what Indigenous people need when it comes to health, for example, Indigenous-controlled health providers and their peak body, the National Aboriginal Community Controlled

Health Organisation are credible sources of guidance.

As another example, if an issue is related to the care of Indigenous children, I would sooner listen to the Secretariat of National Aboriginal and Islander Child Care – the peak body for the care of Indigenous Australian children – than I would a conservative Aboriginal politician. SNAICC is one of the oldest Indigenous peak bodies, championing the rights and protection of Indigenous children for more than forty years. The Secretariat produces an annual report, *Family Matters*, detailing evidence-based solutions that will enable our children to grow up safe, loved and protected.

The most important advice I can give is to not wait for 'all' Indigenous people to support an initiative. If you wait until there is no debate amongst us, you will do nothing and conditions will not improve; the gap will not close.

Use critical thinking to assess what the various Indigenous leaders and groups are saying, and act on what you feel is best, taking into consideration their arguments for or against an idea.

Indigenous people will take your backyard ...

Whenever Indigenous people have been on the cusp of positive change, out it comes, that same old set of warnings that Australians will lose their possessions and privileges; in particular, that Aboriginal people will take their homes and land.

We heard these kinds of fearmongering taunts before Indigenous people won equal wages sixty years ago, and during land rights and Native Title cases. Indigenous people succeeded, and the warnings about backyards being lost, fishermen having nowhere to fish, economies crashing, and separate Aboriginal governments in a divided Australia, never happened and never will.[2] Each of our achievements made a fairer, more united, and prouder country with barely a ripple of change for mainstream Australia. The fears that were whipped up around the Voice would have also evaporated once it took shape if Australians had voted Yes.

$30 billion is spent on 500,000 Indigenous people each year ...

When Tony Abbott was Prime Minister, he appointed a former Labor Party President come Conservative, Warren Mundine, as the Chair of his Indigenous Advisory Council.

As mentioned earlier, Abbott's first budget cut more than $500 million from programs and services that were assisting Indigenous people to improve their lives and their communities. Mundine was Abbott's most vocal Indigenous supporter, often defending the cuts in the media.

In 2016 on the ABC's *Q+A* program, Mundine said that he had met with the Productivity Commission and found that '$30 billion is spent in [the Indigenous] space annually'.[3]

During the referendum campaign in 2023, Tony Abbott repeated the claim, saying that the National Indigenous Australians Agency 'disburses [the same amount] on various Indigenous Australians'.[4]

Mundine was fact checked in 2016.[5] Abbott was fact checked in 2023.[6] Their claims were proven to be false. Yet still, the No campaign spread the lie about the $30 billion Indigenous windfall on their social media pages. This lie was damaging. I heard the number $30 billion bandied around often as a reason to vote No to the Voice. People were told that if Indigenous Australians were already being given so much money why give them more money for a Voice?

In fact, while the Productivity Commission estimated around $30 billion was spent on Indigenous services in 2012–13, that total included mainstream services that all Australians have access to, such as funding for defence, foreign aid, schools and healthcare. Only a small part of that money, around $6 billion, is spent on Indigenous programs and services,[7] and only a trickle of that money reaches people in the communities once myriad other costs, such as administration and other service provider overheads, are taken from it.

They are not a 'real Aborigine' because they aren't black enough ...

The argument about who is a 'real Aboriginal person' ignores the fact that lighter skinned Indigenous people experience racism too. The anonymous text message and examples I shared earlier demonstrate this reality. It also ignores the legacy of cultural genocide and policies to 'breed the colour out'.

It is not for non-Indigenous people to determine who is or is not Indigenous. Indigenous Australians have formal, informal and cultural ways to determine who is part of our community. The formal process, often used by government agencies and community organisations, requires that all three of the following criteria apply:

1. Being of Aboriginal and/or Torres Strait Islander descent
2. Identifying as an Aboriginal and/or Torres Strait Islander person
3. Being accepted as such by the community in which you live, or formerly lived.[8]

Be aware that Bad Actors will go to great lengths to undermine and discredit effective Indigenous advocates and leaders by questioning their Indigenous heritage. This behaviour is often a distraction from the matter at hand.

The lies about 'elite Aboriginals' ...

A person who has worked hard to gain a high level of education, who has years of experience advocating for their people, and who has broken the cycles of poverty and social dysfunction that have surrounded them from childhood – setting a great example – is far from an 'elite' who should not be listened to.

People such as Marcia Langton AO, Tom Calma AO, Noel Pearson, Pat Anderson AO, Pat Turner AM, Peter Yu AM and Napau Pedro Stephen AM are leaders we should respect and listen to. As a matter of course, their views deserve critical analysis too, and that is the process I have followed when researching and writing this book. We should never blindly follow what anyone says without questioning and assessing it.

The argument about 'elites' is similar to when commentators complain about urban Indigenous people advocating for our remote brothers and sisters. This is as ridiculous as saying Australians who live in cities should ignore when farmers are suffering from drought in regional Australia – how un-Australian would that be?

Indigenous people lack initiative, they don't want to work ...

I addressed this matter in chapter 5. In brief, it is a completely false – and racist – point of view. Aboriginal and Torres Strait Islander people work and pay tax like other Australians, while at the same time, we are up against unconscious bias, racism and the debilitating effects of intergenerational trauma, legacy health issues and poverty. This is a sad reality of economic exclusion and the devaluing of caring for Country and culture.

That there are greater numbers of Aboriginal and Torres Strait Islander people who are unemployed and on welfare is a systemic problem – not a matter of race or culture.

When anything that empowers Indigenous people is said to be racist...

Many people argue that any recognition of Indigenous peoples, either symbolic or practical, is dividing Australia by race. But they are ignoring what racism is and how racism, with its harmful effects, can be countered by providing opportunities and empowerment to the minorities who have suffered from it.

As you have read in Part Two, Australia was built on acts of racism against Indigenous people. Racism – the belief that the 'Indigenous race was inferior' – was the excuse for genocide and exclusion. Racism not only harms Indigenous people directly, but it has shaped the nation's Constitution, our systems of law, the distribution of wealth and the geographical locations of our communities. Racism still affects us today.

The Human Rights Commission's definition of racism reminds us that: 'racism includes all the laws, policies, ideologies and barriers that prevent people from experiencing justice, dignity, and equity because of their racial identity. It can come in the form of harassment, abuse or humiliation, violence or intimidating behaviour. However racism also exists in systems and institutions that operate in ways that lead to inequity and injustice.'[9]

An Indigenous Voice, and any other measure that offers justice, dignity and equity for a people who have suffered from racism, is in fact anti-racist. Unifying, not divisive.

Australia treats all people the same ...

The truth is, we don't. Everything in this book, and in the statistics that illustrate the stark differences in outcomes for Indigenous people, confirm that Indigenous people are treated differently from other Australians, and mostly to their detriment.

An individual who treats all people the same, regardless of colour, does not suddenly negate the racism that Indigenous people suffer in Australian society – whether subtle or blatant, individually or systemically, as a distinct minority.

The claim that there are 'no ongoing negative impacts from colonisation' ...

The demonstrably misleading and insulting claim that colonisation has left no negative legacy – because, for example, 'now we have running water' and 'readily available food'[10] – is readily disproved.

'Now we have running water'?

This is an idiotic comment. It is as if the First Peoples were dying of thirst for 65,000 years until the British came along and saved them. Our country has long had some of the most magnificent freshwater springs, waterholes and rivers in the world. Indigenous people had good, plentiful water before white people came here.

Since colonisation, Aboriginal and Torres Strait Islanders across generations have had their water sources poisoned, blocked off and polluted. The fight for access to clean, safe water continues.

Numerous reports have consistently found that dozens of communities have unfit drinking water supplies due to contamination by microbes (bacteria and viruses), nitrates or uranium, with little improvement since 2015.[11]

As recently as 2019, a research paper on drinking water quality found that water supplied to more than 25,000 people in 99 small communities had failed to pass Australian guidelines.[12]

Now we have 'readily available food'?

Before First Nations lands were invaded, the people had free access to fields of native grasses, flowering yams and abundant hunting opportunities; they enjoyed estuaries, rivers and beaches teeming with delicious fishes and molluscs; even the desert was plentiful, with the benefit of tens of thousands of years of accrued knowledge.

To suggest that food security has improved since colonisation is the height of ignorance. The situation in many Indigenous communities is quite the opposite.

Food insecurity is a root cause for much higher rates of chronic disease among Aboriginal and Torres Strait Islander people.[13] Their diets are adversely affected by incredibly high costs. For example, healthy food baskets cost about 20–43 per cent more in remote communities as compared to major cities.[14] In the Aboriginal community of Ramingining, 1 kilogram of Nescafé instant coffee costs as much as $74 and powdered milk costs as much as $10.25.[15] Inconsistent access to power for refrigeration is another factor that makes it near impossible to keep fresh, healthy foods from spoiling. These problems that are unique in Indigenous communities, when combined with unemployment and crowded housing, lead to obesity, high blood cholesterol, poor mental health, excessive alcohol consumption and high blood pressure.

Blackfellas are not looking after their own health ...

I spoke about this with Jaki Adams, a Wuthathi and Yadhaigana woman who works for the Fred Hollows Foundation. The Foundation is a leader in eye health, since its founder and namesake brought eye care to Aboriginal people.

Jaki thought the best way to respond to this particular myth about 'Indigenous privilege' is to offer some insights to the challenges that cause Indigenous adults to be three times more likely to go blind than other Australians; twelve times more likely to have cataracts; and for Australia to be the only high-income country with endemic trachoma (a debilitating eye disease), with no reported cases of trachoma in non-Indigenous Australians.

Let's start with housing. In Indigenous communities, many houses have been built without regard to Indigenous societal ways or the climate and remote conditions. Still today, there are Indigenous communities that don't have clean running water or working taps and therefore no washing facilities.

These housing issues make face, hand and eye hygiene nearly impossible.

The environment is also a factor. There are extreme temperatures in many Indigenous communities that are rapidly worsening with climate change. Housing that was already unsuitable is even less so in these conditions.

In some parts of the bush, there are swarms of sticky little bush flies (*Musca vetustissima*) that will seek the moisture in the eyes of the cleanest of persons, bringing with them the potential to carry harmful bacteria. The flies make the prevention of contagious eye diseases difficult, especially when combined with the housing, water and food security problems, and the lack of services.

I mentioned earlier how a lack of reliable and affordable power affects refrigeration, and therefore the keeping of medicines and healthy perishable food. Unreliable power supply also makes it hard to run air-conditioning systems and other appliances that people in mainstream communities largely take for granted.

Access to health professionals is more difficult too. Indigenous communities have minimal health staff, usually limited to a nurse and rarely a GP. There can also be a lack of equipment, consumables and, again, power and water, with which to deal with patients' variable medical needs. So, people are expected to leave the community and travel hundreds of kilometres to receive medical care. Outside the community, racism and prejudice then impact healthcare. Which brings us to challenges for urban First Nations people.

Apart from Indigenous-controlled health providers, services may not be culturally responsive or welcoming in towns and cities. The examples of uninformed decisions or racism leading to people being misdiagnosed, sometimes fatally,[16] are far too numerous. This poor record has damaged many Indigenous people's trust in the health system, which leads to delays in diagnosis and care.

Racism also negatively affects the attraction, recruitment, retention and leadership opportunities of the Indigenous health workforce, vital to increasing uptake of health services.

Before colonisation, Aboriginal and Torres Strait Islander people likely lived full and healthy lives. We had our medicines and our healers. We ate healthy foods. Our children and our Elders were cared for collectively by the community. The health disparities are another legacy of colonisation, poor policy and negligence.

All Indigenous people get free university degrees, free cars and interest-free loans ...

Indigenous Australians are not getting free university degrees.

There are myriad reasons why some Australians receive government support or scholarships to gain a university education.[17] This could be because of skills shortages in an industry or region, or to overcome the challenges that are holding some minorities back.

The claims that Aboriginal and Torres Strait Islander people get free cars is false. This misconception may have come from racism: when people cannot fathom how Indigenous people could possibly own a nice car. Indigenous Australians do not get interest free loans either. This is an out and out lie.

Aboriginal and Torres Strait Islander people have a vote, they don't need special representation such as a Voice …

Most politicians, and especially federal ministers, have rarely visited remote Aboriginal communities, if at all. The political reality is brutally clear: there are few votes to gain from a small minority, many of whom live in hard-to-reach places.

The infrequent visits, at times unannounced and as short as a photo shoot, and the misrepresentation of what the people have to say over many decades, cause low levels of community trust in bureaucratic and political decision-makers.

There are other ways that people can have their voices heard by decision-makers, but this is different for Indigenous people. If you live hundreds of kilometres from the nearest town, with unreliable power supply and internet; if you have one car shared amongst multiple families, with few who have a driver's licence; if the fuel for the car is almost three times more expensive than it is in the city; if you are looking after old people, who aren't that old really but who are suffering from diseases that could have been preventable in their youth; and if your youth are disaffected, bored, with few prospects for higher education and employment, who are carrying the burdens of generations of trauma, how can you organise effective representation to improve all of the above for the health and prosperity of your people?

Australians might not be ready for a constitutionally enshrined Voice to Parliament anytime soon, but it will be achieved eventually – because it makes so much sense. In the meantime, we must continue our advocacy to help Indigenous people to be heard, whether it be via legislation, reserved senate seats like Māori people have in Aotearoa New Zealand, or through a treaty outcome.

Indigenous people were primitive and would have been invaded anyway ...

As adults – hopefully even as children – we understand that just because someone else is likely to commit a wrongdoing, doesn't mean we have a good reason to beat them to it.

It really does not matter if the French, or the Dutch, or any of the other colonial powers of the time might have invaded First Nations if the British didn't. That just does not stack up as an argument to invade, simply for their own further empowerment.

It is worth thinking about why Indigenous Australians were out-gunned and overrun by the British. Were Europeans really the more intelligent civilisation for having developed weapons for mass killing? In hindsight, who had the better way of life – those who dug up, cut down, burnt and polluted the natural world, or those who lived in harmony with it?

We could learn from Indigenous ways of being: for environmental sustainability, for social cohesion, and for dispute resolution.

Yes, Indigenous people still had violence. There were feuds and there was war. But they waged war in ways that did not damage the earth, and with comparatively less bloodshed. They also already had an enduring capacity for peaceful co-existence and for respecting each other's boundaries.

That First Nations were less armed and less ready for war against the British does not justify what followed when the first settlers arrived, any more than a person deserves to be battered by a bully, just because the bully is stronger.

Colonisation was legitimate ...

The British, and then citizens of the Australian Commonwealth, broke both First Nations and British laws when they raped, tortured, massacred, abducted or enslaved Indigenous peoples.

Whenever Aboriginal people acted in self-defence, or to protect their families, communities and territory, the settlers, in bands of vigilantes, and the state, took disproportionate revenge.

You can imagine how flexible the law would have been for the leaders of the colonies, charged with the expansion of British interests, and motivated by ambitions for prestige and wealth. Think about how little a Black life would have mattered to a convict settler who had served hard time, with land of their own to build wealth, a cup full of drink and a head full of trauma. Or what about free settlers who had arrived in the new colony, having endured the months-long journey at sea?

Could a bunch of First Nations people possibly negotiate with a settler who, from their own perspective, had risked all for the promise of land and their dreams of making a fortune – and who had a ready excuse that Indigenous people were inferior?

In more modern times, right to this day, a way to see continuing injustice against Indigenous people is to understand the inexcusably disproportionate number of Indigenous deaths in custody. Since the results of the Royal Commission into Aboriginal Deaths in Custody were published in 1991, there have been more than 500 Indigenous deaths in custody.[18] Families are still crying out for justice.

A treaty will ruin Australia...

When Aboriginal and Torres Strait Islander people talk about wanting a treaty, we are seeking an agreement about how the state will recognise it exists on stolen land.

A treaty would help Australia to catch up with its peers. Among comparable settler colonial nations, such as Canada, Aotearoa New Zealand and the USA, our country is the only one that does not have a treaty with Indigenous people, or a form of recognition in the Constitution.[19]

Many Australians have been fed the lie that a treaty will harm them in some way. This goes back to the old scare tactic that Australians might lose their land to Indigenous people. We should help all Australians understand that First Nations people cannot force an outcome that the country would not accept. A treaty is only possible if the greater power – the Commonwealth Parliament, with their great resources and political might, agrees to its content, and passes legislation to enact it.

The success of a treaty (by success, I mean an outcome that will be to the satisfaction of First Nations people) will depend on how actively the Australian public will support the First Nations' claims.

∞∞∞

I have no doubt that most Australians want a fair and respectful nation, where our children can expect to be treated justly in a democracy that is thriving, and everyone has opportunities to prosper. These aspirations are under threat because of the challenges we collectively face, including the cost of living, growing inequality, unaffordable housing, and a rejection of the modest request that we should listen to Indigenous Australians.

The observations I have made in this chapter remind us that to achieve a peaceful and just society, we must work together to overcome fear, misunderstanding and hate. When we create groups, organisations and safe spaces to teach and practise critical thinking, nurture patience and understanding, and fight against bigotry and racism – and when we stop to listen and invite others in – we can turn the tide, bringing truth and hope to our country.

CHAPTER 9

A guide to protocol, awareness and respect

A good friend Jade Ritchie, a Gooreng Gooreng woman, led many Yes campaign gatherings and meetings with mob in community. She helped me to compile some answers to questions about protocol that we were often asked as we travelled around the country in 2023. We thought this guidance would be valuable because people want to be respectful, but sometimes they don't know what to do or not to do.

This list won't cover every question that people have and, as in any large group, opinions will vary. Other First Nations people might offer different answers. But I hope that what follows in this chapter will help to bring about cooperation as we work together toward peace and justice for First Nations people.

Respecting our Elders

We always acknowledge and pay respect to our Elders. In Aboriginal and Torres Strait Islander culture, our Elders are valued and respected for their role in caring for children when they are young and guiding them as they grow older. They are a source of wisdom for our communities, central to dispute resolution and custodians of our lore and law. We also pay our respects to our Elders because throughout their lives, even in the most difficult conditions, they strived to create a better life for our future generations.

The title Uncle or Aunty

It is best to not just assume that an Aboriginal or Torres Strait Islander person should be called Uncle or Aunty because they look elderly. These titles are not determined by age alone.

Observe how others refer to someone, or how they refer to themselves and then follow their lead. If there have been no cues, refer to them as you would any other person.

In some cultures, there may be a language name to respectfully refer to an Elder. In the Torres Strait, for example, the word for Uncle is 'Awa', and the word for Aunty is 'Ama'. A senior Elder may be referred to as 'Athé' for Grandfather, or 'Aka' for Grandmother.

Welcome to Country ceremonies

Incorporating Acknowledgement of Country and Welcome to Country into meetings, conferences and other events is a cultural protocol that demonstrates respect for the Traditional Owners of the area.

The ceremonies are both customary, continuing a practice that began thousands of years ago, and an important modern statement, celebrating the survival of First Nations people and culture since colonisation.

There is a difference between a Welcome to Country and an Acknowledgement of Country. Only Traditional Owners, or a group authorised by Traditional Owners, can perform a Welcome to Country. To organise a Welcome to Country, it is best to contact a local Aboriginal Land Council or Native Title representative body for the area where the event is being held and ask if it is appropriate to have a Welcome to Country at your event. If they agree that it is, then ask them to suggest someone who can do it for you. It is advisable to do this well in advance of the event, as that person might not be available on short notice. As with any service, a person's or organisation's time and expertise should attract payment.

A Welcome to Country ceremony is usually held at the start of a formal event or large gathering. It can take many forms including traditional songs, dances, smoking ceremonies, and/or a speech.

Acknowledgement of Country

An Acknowledgement of Country is an act of respect for the Traditional Owners of the land and the broader First Nations population that anyone can do at the beginning of an event or speech.

If a Welcome to Country is not given at an event, then there should always be an Acknowledgement of Country. This should come from an appropriately senior person, rather than an Indigenous staff member or participant who, as can often happen, is only asked to do it as an afterthought.

If there has been a Welcome to Country performed by the traditional custodians in an earlier ceremony, or an Acknowledgement of Country on behalf of the gathering, there is no obligation for non-Indigenous people to repeat an Acknowledgement every time they speak.

Reconciliation Australia offers the following guidance on sets of wording:

'I'd like to begin by acknowledging the Traditional Owners of the land on which we meet today. I would also like to pay my respects to Elders past and present.'

I'd like to begin by acknowledging the Traditional Owners of the land on which we meet today, the (people) of the (nation) and pay my respects to Elders past and present.

There is no suggestion that 'emerging' or 'future' Elders should be mentioned. Such a reference is frowned upon by much of the Aboriginal and Torres Strait Islander community because becoming a respected Elder is not an honour that can be guaranteed or expected before it is earned and it is granted according to cultural protocols. For more about this, you can read Professor Megan Davis' essay in the July 2020 edition of *The Monthly*.[1]

Social media dos and don'ts

Social media can be a helpful tool to share information and activities with your friends and followers. But try not to spend too much time online when you could be out there doing real-life advocacy.

Bad Actors have been highly effective online. You can fight online disinformation and fear mongering by using short, factual posts and comments, including links to any evidence to back your claims. Also, for those of you with a streak of creativity and who are skilled at making TikToks, Instagram reels and the like on social media platforms, you can help with truth-telling and myth-busting. Use your initiative and innovation to create content that gets eyeballs on fun facts about how great First Nations culture is and how ridiculous the Bad Actors are. Satire, when done well, such as by the brilliant people behind *The Shot* and the *Betoota Advocate*, works a treat.

The most important advice about social media is to avoid getting into a comment war with racists and trolls. They want to waste your time, intimidate you into silence and create open conflict. Give them nothing other than your short facts, a link to some evidence, if you can, and move on.

Beware of inadvertently pushing misinformation on to a wider audience by blindly sharing posts that poke at your emotions. Even if you are sharing a Bad Actor's tweet or post to disagree with it, you are helping that post reach more people.

Everything on social media should always be taken with a grain of salt. Fact check and check again, and ensure that you are using a trusted source, as discussed earlier in this book.

Finally, use the privacy settings to limit who can see you and who you can see if need be. Block the trolls and the racists after you report them to the social media platform provider. And share the information in this section with your friends and family if they are on social media.

Tackling racism

It is essential that we actively fight racism by calling it out. If we don't, our inaction sends a message that racism is acceptable. What we walk past, we accept.

There are some excellent resources available to help us learn about and address racist conduct. There is also legislation that prohibits racism, including the *Racial Discrimination Act 1975*, in particular Section 18c: Offensive behaviour because of race, colour or national or ethnic origin.[2]

'Racism. It Stops With Me' is a national campaign that provides the tools and resources to stamp out racism. Visit itstopswithme.humanrights.gov.au.

Complaints about racism can be made to the Australian Human Rights Commission: humanrights.gov.au/complaints. You can phone the Commission for advice on 1300 656 419 or (02) 9284 9600.

Joining a union is a great line of defence against racism. Unions are ready and organised to back members up should a matter arise.

If a racist incident happens online, you can report it to the Office of the eSafety Commissioner. Collect and preserve the evidence by taking a screenshot of the offensive post or content, and make your report here: esafety.gov.au/report

You can also record your incident on the First Nations Racism Register. The register provides a simple and secure way for people to report or 'call out' incidents of racism and discrimination toward First Nations people. The purpose of the initiative is to collect information on racism, including how it is experienced, how often it is occurring, and the impact it is having on people. This information will inform evidence-based research that enables reporting on racism and its impacts, inform anti-racism action, support the response of First Nations organisations and leaders, and educate the wider community. Find out more at callitout.com.au

Reconciliation Action Plans

Reconciliation Action Plans (RAPs) can guide organisations to contribute to the national reconciliation movement. They can provide an accredited way for companies to make an impact by setting internal targets for such goals as increased Indigenous employment or procurement spend, as well as participation in movements like the referendum campaign and truth-telling.

It is important that a RAP is more than lip service. RAPs should be properly resourced as a budget priority. If a company does not put both human and financial resources towards their RAP commitments, then it is likely they have no intention of implementing them.

Staff play an important role in keeping a company accountable. So get involved in your organisation's RAP committee and participate in activities. If your employer has a RAP, become familiar with it and ensure the commitments are enacted and not tokenistic. If your company doesn't have a RAP, find out why, and invite them to start the process. For more information go to reconciliation.org.au

Visit Aboriginal and Torres Strait Islander communities

Visiting Aboriginal and Torres Strait Islander communities is a great way to immerse yourself in our culture. However, it is best to do this when invited or as part of a cultural tourism package.

There are hundreds of First Nations groups, not just in the bush but in the cities as well, such as Redfern in Sydney, with hundreds of unique languages. Be aware of this diversity. Customs and protocols will vary from place to place. Also, in remote communities, English may be a third or fourth language.

A guide who is a Traditional Owner can be a great help if they are available. Listen carefully to any instructions they may give before and during your visit.

If you are permitted to walk Country, as a rule, do not remove rocks or any other objects without the permission of Traditional Owners. Disturbing cultural sites is also prohibited by Australian law, so be careful not to trespass on areas that are sacred. Restricted areas may include around trees, hills and waterholes. Some areas may also be restricted for either male or female visitors. Take notice of any signs and obey any instructions. And if you don't know, ask.

In some communities, you will need to dress appropriately:
- wear loose-fitting and long style (below the knee) clothing including shorts, skirts, pants, trousers and dresses
- wear shirts or t-shirts with sleeves
- if you are invited to swim, you may swim with your clothes on, or with a t-shirt and shorts covering your swimming costume

- in case you are invited to sit on the ground, you should wear clothing that will not cause embarrassment or discomfort
- cotton garments rather than synthetic fibres are recommended in warm and humid conditions as they allow the skin to breathe.

There are restrictions on taking photographs in some communities. Taking photographs of children will require the permission of their parents or guardians. If you are considering using your photographs for publicity purposes or in publications, you should also obtain written permission from the subjects.

Be aware that some Aboriginal and Torres Strait Islander communities have chosen to ban alcohol in their community. We recommend not drinking at all during a visit.

Respect should be an inherent part of your interaction with everybody within the community. In many communities, it is considered rude to ask lots of questions. If you have a lot to ask, you may learn you are asking too much because you will not get answers. Try not to be offended if this happens. It is important to observe others and follow their lead to avoid embarrassment. This includes protocol around shaking hands and eye contact.

Respectful and ethical commercial engagement

In chapter 6 we discussed the importance of meaningful economic participation. There are many ways in which you can support this, whether as an individual, an employee or a business owner.

The Uluru Statement describes our culture as a gift to our country, and certainly Indigenous Cultural Intellectual Property has proven to be highly sought after. However, our culture is often monetised by outsiders and rarely attributed correctly or appropriately valued. It is important to be aware of the large-scale cultural theft that takes place across the nation and ensure you don't accidentally contribute to it.

Beware of Black cladding, which is when non-Indigenous businesses gain contracts that are subject to Indigenous procurement policies by using an Indigenous entity or individual as a front.

A useful resource to assist in navigating complex laws, relationships and protocols, including the practice of Black cladding, is a book written by my cousin, Dr Terri Janke, called *True Tracks*.

Terri is an award-winning lawyer and leading international authority on Indigenous cultural and intellectual property. She is the owner and Solicitor Director of Terri Janke and Company. Her book is a must-read for anyone who wants to understand ethical commercial engagement with Aboriginal and Torres Strait Islander people.

∞∞∞

By now you should be energised with hope, moved by the good and the bad throughout Australian history, wisened up to truth and lies and familiar with First Nations people and some of our significant protocols. What comes next is action. Without action, how do we ever turn the page?

CHAPTER 10

Overcoming uncertainty and fear with familiarity

Today, more Australians than ever before are learning about First Nations history and culture, and we must not take this progress for granted. We should each find a way to help increase the momentum and recognise that we still have a long way to go.

In chapter 7, we explored how Bad Actors used the lack of familiarity that many Australians have with Indigenous people to their advantage during the referendum campaign. They created a sense of suspicion, as if Indigenous Australians are strangers who cannot be trusted. Voter uncertainty made the No campaign slogan effective: 'If you don't know, vote No.'

But around six million voters resisted the No campaign tactics. They dismissed the lies and saw through the obfuscation because they knew us.

There is power in familiarity. It protects people from fear.

Young people are an excellent example. Schools are now practising Acknowledgements of Country, teaching First Nations languages, and using the work of Indigenous authors and creatives in their lessons. I believe this is why a majority of the youngest cohort of Australian voters wrote 'Yes'.

Educating young people about Aboriginal and Torres Strait Islander cultures is an important national project, and it can have a beneficial impact on the mental health of Aboriginal and Torres Strait Islander children as well.

I was taught little about Indigenous history and culture in general back when I was at school, more than thirty years ago. But it was different at home. I was fortunate to have learnt about my Torres Strait Islander culture while practising traditional dancing, gathering traditional foods, and cooking for ceremonies with my dad and community.

Because I had a firm grasp of my identity, and because I had excellent cultural mentors and role models, I have been able to resist the comments and insinuations that Indigenous people hear, such as, 'You must be lazy because you are Black', 'You will be a failure because you are Black', and 'You are not Black enough to be speaking up for the Blacks.' Being familiar with my culture built a shield for me that kept the Bad Actors from corrupting my mental health. That shield is made of knowledge, love and pride.

I know of some Indigenous Australians who have been less fortunate, though. Those who from an early age, have had little to no connection with their culture and people. They have struggled throughout their lives to deal with the pain of not feeling accepted – not by Indigenous or non-Indigenous groups. In some cases, they believed the racist taunts they heard about themselves. Their mental health was torn apart. This is why I believe that Aboriginal and Torres Strait Islander people must have opportunities to make lasting, positive connections with their people and culture, starting from early childhood.

ooooo

Each one of us has the power to expand Australia's consciousness of who Aboriginal and Torres Strait Islander people are, by introducing their wonderful culture to others. You can give our fellow Australians the gift of resilience against the lies they too often hear.

I ask that you talk with your children, your friends and your family about our proud, ancient and ongoing culture, and its unique place in the world. Show them that First Nations people continue to be a valuable source of wisdom, knowledge and connection to our continent. Help them to become familiar with the truth.

Before you get out there, however, it is important to recognise that not every Indigenous Australian has the time to be your personal educator. Be respectful in your approach. Make sure you value our time and expertise. For this reason, the following tips focus on ways to become familiar with First Nations cultures and history through methods and in settings that are easily accessible and well established.

Ways to find out about our culture

Here are some ways that you can engage with Aboriginal and Torres Strait Islander culture.

Books

At the end of this book is a 'Useful resources' list, which gives details about well-respected and informative publications written by Indigenous and non-Indigenous authors. Also, ask at your local bookshop about their range of books by Indigenous authors. You'll find works across many genres for children and adults.

As well as reading them yourself, you can lend or give these books as gifts to help the people around you become familiar with Aboriginal and Torres Strait Island stories and culture. Don't forget to follow up and ask if they have read the book yet. You might also ask if they have any questions or would like to discuss what they read. This could lead to important conversations, and you also may want to suggest other books they can read to fill any gaps.

You can follow @blackfulla_bookclub on Instagram to find out about the latest books by First Nations authors.

Indigenous art

Displaying works by Aboriginal and Torres Strait Islander artists in your home, your business or as murals on buildings helps people to become familiar with our culture. You could buy an artwork for a friend, a family member or colleague, and in doing so, you might help them to understand the story that goes with it. Include the artist's biography and photo with the gift.

Before you buy an artwork, though, it is important to enquire about its authenticity. If you are a business engaging an artist, check the credentials of the artist and the gallery that represents them.

There are a number of initiatives that help consumers identify ethical and authentic art sources, such as Indigenous Art Code, indigenousartcode.org

Museum and gallery exhibitions curated by First Nations people are a wonderful window to Indigenous culture. As well as showing artefacts and art, many exhibitions explore the history of our struggle, and through works by artists such as Richard Bell, Daniel Boyd and Fiona Foley, you may contemplate contemporary statements about justice and sovereignty.

Documentaries and films

There is a wide range of movies, TV series and documentaries that cover historic and modern Aboriginal and Torres Strait Islander experiences. As well as watching the movies, you can also follow the careers of some of the brilliant Indigenous pioneers and emerging talent in the industry, such as directors, producers, film writers and actors. They include Warwick Thornton, Rachel Perkins, Steven McGregor, Gary Hamaguchi, Tyson Perkins, Danielle MacLean, Adam Thompson, Darlene Johnson, Deb Mailman, Ngaire Pigram, Luke Carroll, Robbie Collins, Quaden Bayles, Madeleine Maddon, Miranda Tapsell, Nakkiah Lui, Ernie Dingo, Leah Purcell and Justin Rhys Grant – and many, many more.

Performing arts

Indigenous performers, choreographers, directors and playwrights are world class. A couple of examples are Deborah Cheetham Fraillon AO and Wesley Enoch AM.

Deborah is a Yorta Yorta soprano, composer and educator who established the national not-for-profit company, Short Black Opera, in 2009, assisting Indigenous singers to develop their careers. In 2010, Cheetham Fraillon produced the first Indigenous opera, *Pecan Summer*. A magical moment so far in her career was the sold-out premiere of her work, *Eumeralla, a war requiem for peace*, sung entirely in the dialects of the Gunditjmara language. It was performed on Country in October 2018, and then at Hamer Hall in Melbourne with the Melbourne Symphony Orchestra in June 2019.

Quandamooka, Ngugi and Kaantju man Wesley Enoch is one of the greats in the performing arts in Australia. I first met Wesley soon after the Uluru Statement was created in 2017. Since then I have witnessed the playwright and artistic director's positive influence across the arts, and in particular, his generous mentorship of many a young up-and-comer. His works are true to Indigenous ways, such as the plays *The 7 Stages of Grieving* co-written with Deborah Mailman, and *The Story of the Miracles at Cookie's Table*. A particularly powerful story that he directed was Jane Harrison's *Stolen* at the Ilbijerri Theatre in Melbourne. *Stolen* follows the lives of five Aboriginal children who were taken from their families. At the Sorrento Writers Festival in 2023, he told me that he is 'especially interested in bringing the stories that have been suppressed or forgotten to the fore – writing onto the public record our stories, our way'.

A Torres Strait Islander playwright, producer and actor, whose work I have enjoyed since I discovered the wonder of theatre, is Nakkiah Lui. She demonstrates the power of First Nations humour, making audiences laugh and cry, and hang on to their seat in suspense, all while challenging them to think more deeply about race, class and politics. Her award-winning play, *Black is the new White*, has also been published as a book.

Without a doubt, performing island dancing for my own families and the broader community at schools and public events gave me the confidence to go on and fight for social justice. I have witnessed many creative, young Aboriginal and Torres Strait Islander people find their wings through dance. Some of them went from performing at home to graduating from the National Aboriginal and Islander Skills Development Association, and go on to join outstanding dance companies, such as Karul Projects, Bangarra Dance Theatre, BlakDance and Brolga Dance Academy.

Brolga Dance Academy is based in Redfern, Sydney. Founded in 2020 by Gamilaroi and Murrawari woman Jodie Choolburra-Welsh, who was born and raised on Gadigal land in Redfern, the academy received the Sydney City Business of the Year in Performing Arts Award in 2023. The academy is now connecting children to First Nations dancing in communities well beyond Sydney.

Karul was started by Minjugbal-Yugambeh/Wiradjuri/Ni-Vanuatu man Thomas ES Kelly and Kaurna/Narungga/Ngarindjerri woman

Taree Sansbury in 2017. The company has been touring the country with a show called *Silence*, which is very much about truth telling.

I have enjoyed Bangarra Dance Theatre's work twice at the Sydney Opera House. Both times were memorable. Their professional Aboriginal and Torres Strait Islander performers have been sharing culture with audiences for over 30 years.

BlakDance was established in 2005 and is based on Turrbal and Yuggera Country at the Judith Wright Centre. Their creative developments are performed in studio and on Country.

The following are a few more directors and producers to note. Isaac Drandic is a Noongar playwright and director who is working on creating a theatre piece based on my book about First Nations perspectives on fatherhood, *Dear Son*. He has worked closely with playwright, Trawlwoolway man Nathan Maynard, on a masterpiece called *37*, centred on Aussie Rules football, and *At What Cost?*, which focuses on Indigenous identity and history on the lands that are now called Tasmania.

Andrea James is a Yorta Yorta/Gunaikurnai creative producer. Together with Anyupa Butcher and Sammy Tjapanangka Butcher, she co-wrote the highly entertaining rock 'n' roll extravaganza based on the iconic Warumpi Band, *Big Name, No Blankets*. An interesting new work she created and directed is *Sunshine Super Girl*, telling Evonne Goolagong's heartwarming story.

Finally, I will mention two more theatre companies. If you are in Perth, check out the Yirra Yaakin Aboriginal Theatre Company. They produce award-winning theatre that has a focus on education for young Australians. The second is Moogahlin Performing Arts, based in Redfern on Gadigal land. In 2024 they staged *The Visitors* written by Jane Harrison and directed by Wesley Enoch.

Music

Where does one start when it comes to Aboriginal and Torres Strait Islander music? Music is how we have kept stories alive from millennia ago to today. From the traditional to the contemporary, from rap to opera, there are brilliant Indigenous artists. In some regions, our mob love country music, in others, they smash out reggae, pop, rap, or rock 'n' roll. To help you to compile an Always was, Always will be playlist, I have put together a guide to First Nations musicians at the back of the book.

Indigenous festivals and events

Festivals are an opportunity to become immersed in both modern and traditional First Nations cultures. As I've mentioned, theatre productions and exhibitions by Indigenous creatives can be informative and thought-provoking. Live music festivals such the Treaty Day Out in Victoria are brilliant as well.

I have learnt a lot by attending local festivals, such as the Freedom Day Festival that celebrates the Gurindji Wave Hill Walk-Off in Kalkarindji and Daguragu, and the Garma Festival on Yolŋu land. In the Torres Strait Islands, the greatest experience I have ever had at a festival is the Winds of Zenadth Cultural Festival. The colours, the passion and the innovative Island-style dancing, performed across consecutive days and nights on Waiben/Thursday Island, is an unforgettable immersion into Torres Strait culture.

You can also find events such as markets and storytelling gatherings that have been organised by local Indigenous groups and their friends in towns and cities. They are a cost-effective and entertaining way to introduce friends and family to Indigenous culture. These local initiatives need our support, so if you can, you may want to contribute financially or by volunteering to help make these events a success.

Respect and become familiar with our languages

Many Australians are now using traditional names for cities, towns and features around the country, such as kunanyi/Mount Wellington (Tas), and you can use the traditional place name when sending mail with Australia Post. To find out more about First Nations languages, visit the General Interest page of the First Languages Australia website. School teachers might find the notes on the Gambay Map site useful.

Ngarrngga School Curriculum Resources

Ngarrngga, pronounced Naarn-ga, is a program that provides innovative curriculum and professional development resources made by educators for educators, in collaboration with Indigenous knowledge experts from the Faculty of Education, Indigenous Studies Unit and Indigenous Knowledge Institute at The University of Melbourne.

Visit ngarrngga.org for more information.

Cultural awareness workshops

Cultural awareness courses and workshops are a great way to become familiar with First Nations culture. You can do them as an individual, or as a group, workplace or organisation. Your workplace's Reconciliation Action Plan (RAP) and your company's policies might support a decision to engage in an awareness program if you raise this idea with your colleagues.

The Australian Institute of Aboriginal and Islander Studies runs an online program called Core Cultural learning. Its ten modules explore First Nations peoples and issues 'to enhance your cultural understanding; gain a deeper sense of self-awareness and critical reflection; and enhance your personal and professional capacity to engage respectfully and effectively in an intercultural context'.[1]

You may also find local courses that are run by Traditional Owners and Indigenous businesses.

Buy Blak

When you 'buy blak' you are participating in an economy that familiarises you not just with Indigenous products, but with cultural values and customary systems that underpin how we do business.

There are over 17,000 Indigenous businesses registered today across a very wide range of industries, including construction, healthcare and social services, professional services, administration, manufacturing, transport, retail, agriculture, arts, tourism and education.

Volunteer

Keep your eye out for opportunities to volunteer at Indigenous festivals and events. You may also volunteer to lend a hand to service providers and Indigenous programs such as Australians for Native Title and Reconciliation (ANTAR) antar.org.au, Community First Development communityfirstdevelopment.org.au, and the state Reconciliation organisations.

ooooo

These suggestions are just some of the many ways you and your family and friends can learn more about our culture and history. As you read books by Indigenous authors, attend events, watch films and so on, tell others about them. That way, the important and respectful discussions that started in the referendum campaign of 2023 will keep going.

CHAPTER 11

What's next – starting today

Mayilema is the Larrakia season when the heavy tropical heat is slowly pushed out by dry, cool mornings. As if defying the shift in the weather from the wet to the dry, the afternoons feature angry 'knock-em-down' storms, named for the strong gusts that can lay the long spear grass flat.

Mayilema brought her winds of change in April this year. It was a good time to take my son Will to my favourite fishing place at night. We went in my small dinghy, equipped with the bamboo spear we'd made together and a spotlight. Our target fish was zaber, my people's word for garfish, which are found in the shallows of the reef.

As I motored away from the estuary where we launched the boat, the familiar salty truffle smell of the sea enlivened my seafaring instincts. Turning the boat toward the dark shape of an island where the reef lay, I looked back at my son who was sitting astern. His silhouette was outlined by the phosphorescence in the dinghy's wake. I smiled, though he could not see me. He was gazing at the stars ahead, probably wondering, as I once did, how he might one day find his way to the reef on his own.

Arriving at the reef almost an hour later, we prepared the spotlight as I gave Will some final instructions. Soon he would step up to the bow for his first try at night spearing.

As we moved slowly across the shallows of the reef, we could hear the zaber jumping about the boat, sometimes hitting the hull. A few leapt onboard, catching themselves. But when struck by the bright light, the fish tend to swim steady, a prime target for the skilful fisher or good practice for an eager boy's spear.

The reef at night is teeming with life, from the plentiful but unseen micro-organisms such as plankton and bacteria; the soft sponges, anemone and corals separated by fields of seagrass; the tiddly prawns, dancing crabs, small fish, big fish and giant grouper; the grass-feeding dugongs and turtles; to the ever-patrolling meat hungry sharks – hammerheads, tigers and black-tips. Occasionally we see crocodiles, their eyes glowing red well before their dark and menacing shadow is upon us. There is a croc out there who is as large as our boat.

In Aboriginal and Torres Strait Islander culture, we teach our children sustainability from the moment they are born. They learn kinship and respect for their totems. We all play our part in an intricate web of custodianship. Our societies are not superior to the ecosystem, we are part of it. Balance and harmony depend on every living thing playing its role.

The reef truly is a magnificent place to behold when the night is briefly peeled back with a spotlight. Peering through the still surface is like observing the Earth's many civilisations and cultures, the intricacies and beauty of life and death from the viewpoint of the stars. The varying abilities and capacities of the living creatures around a reef make them the wonder they are.

Australia is like the reef. A reef among countless others in the world. If we don't play our part, balance is lost. If any of the parts take more than their share, if we allow wanton destruction or greed, inevitably, all else will fail.

We must act to restore balance to our country.

A formula to achieve justice and recognition

The formula to achieve justice and recognition for Aboriginal and Torres Strait Islander people is quite simple. First, we need to create the political will for change. Then we need to take action – that involves individuals and organisations, including corporations, unions and religious groups – so that governments will establish good policies. The final part of the equation is consistency. There will be no overnight closing of the gap. Justice and recognition will take time.

$$\text{PEOPLE POWER} + \text{ORGANISATIONS ACTING} +$$
$$\text{GOOD GOVERNMENT POLICIES}$$
$$\times \text{CONSISTENCY}$$
$$=$$
$$\text{JUSTICE AND RECOGNITION}$$

The following is a guide to what you may want to do next, starting today. I have written it in a way that will help you see where your actions will fit into the formula.

Though I could never provide a complete list of actions, I have done my best to offer a wide range of suggestions. I hope you'll find some that suit your personality and lifestyle and that you can fit in among the other commitments in your life. Do a few of them, do them all, do them differently – and always aim to bring people with you.

The next time we have a chance to change the nation for the better with a single vote, the almost 4 per cent, who became 40 per cent in

2023, could become 98 per cent of voters in the country, as it was when Australians voted in the referendum in 1967.

People power

1   Continue conversations

This is the first and most important action. If you were a Yes supporter who took action in the referendum, continue to speak to people as if the campaign were still at stake. If you were not, and you are only learning about these matters, tell others about your journey to becoming informed.

Use the insights and advice in chapters 7 and 8.

2   Familiarity

Use the suggestions in chapter 9 to help you become familiar with Aboriginal and Torres Strait Islander culture, history and contemporary issues, and try to bring people with you.

3   Change place names and memorials

You might organise a campaign in your local area to change the name of a place, to update a memorial, or to generally improve the visible recognition of the Traditional Owners.

As an excellent example, watch young Australians Lionel and Ella Kennedy online explaining how they wrote to the local council, consulted with Dharug Elder, Aunty Lyn Martin, and the Indigenous advisory council that she co-chairs, and then successfully changed a memorial to include an acknowledgement of the Traditional Owners.

An example of a recent place name change is when Fraser Island, the world's largest sand island 300km north of Brisbane in

Queensland, had its Butchulla name restored – K'Gari.

4 Acknowledgement of Country on your property

Your front fence is the perfect place to put up an Acknowledgement of Country sign. If you have taken down your 'Yes' corflute, this would be the place to put it. You might fly Aboriginal and Torres Strait Islander flags, or paint our colours as well. Let's further normalise the recognition of Aboriginal and Torres Strait Islander land, and promote conversations at the same time.

An Aboriginal business that sells Acknowledgement of Country plaques is Kinya Lerrk (Wemba Wemba for 'women coming together'). I am sure there are other Indigenous businesses that sell similar products, and local Indigenous artists you might engage.

5 Truth-telling about massacres in your local area

An impactful action that contributes to bringing the truth of the past to light is when non-Indigenous communities work with First Nations people to memorialise massacres in local areas.

An example is the Myall Creek Massacre memorial. The non-Indigenous side of the campaign began in 1965 when Len Payne, from the town of Bingara in New South Wales, proposed the erection of a memorial to the Bingara Aboriginal people whose ancestors were slaughtered. His proposal was vehemently opposed, but Payne memorialised the event regardless, laying a wreath at the site annually until his death in 1993.

It wasn't until 10 June 2000 that memorial was dedicated. Now hundreds of Australians visit it each year, thanks to the combined efforts of the local Aboriginal community led by Elder Sue

Blacklock, and their non-Indigenous friends.

Another example is the memorial near the remote South Australian town of Elliston. The two stone plinths on the edge of a cliff mark what is known as the 'Massacre of Waterloo Bay', where between twenty and 200 Aboriginal people were driven off a cliff. Similar to the Myall Creek memorial, it took many decades to overcome protests from those non-Indigenous people who did not want to see recognition of the horrific event. They argued that using the word 'massacre' on a memorial would be divisive, that they may be liable to pay compensation for what happened, and that the Aboriginal people will never be satisfied. As so often happens, none of these claims came true when the Traditional Owners and their supporters gained the recognition they sought. Instead, visitors now take a detour especially to visit the simple stones at a cliff's edge in Waterloo Bay.

You should always expect opposition as you take these actions. But if you build a team to run the campaign, find the evidence, work together and persevere, you will succeed.

6   *Truth-telling about First Nations achievement*

We should do much more than memorialise the worst aspects of Australian history. Indigenous knowledge, places and moments of communities coming together should be shared and celebrated nationally.

Share what you know about our wonderful Indigenous science, bush foods and medicines. Tell people about one of the oldest examples of aquaculture and hydraulic engineering in the world: Budj Bim, the Gunditjmara eel traps in Victoria, are around 6,600 years old. Mark special anniversaries, such as the Pilbara Strike, Gurindji Wave Hill Walk-Off, and the anniversary of Cathy

Freeman winning the women's 400m race at the 2000 Olympic Games in Sydney.

Don't wait for NAIDOC Week. Celebrate Aboriginal and Torres Strait Islander achievement every day.

7 *Show up for justice and recognition*

When you attend festivals and other events that showcase and celebrate Indigenous cultures, and when you take part in marches that are calling for positive change or raising awareness about terrible injustices, you are helping to highlight the issues. People Power is vital to raising awareness and influencing governments. Stand side by side with Aboriginal and Torres Strait Islander people. It lifts our hopes when Australians care enough to challenge the unacceptable status quo.

8 *Join the Raise the Age campaign*

In many parts of Australia, juvenile detention centres are filled almost entirely with Aboriginal and Torres Strait Islander children, and they can be as young as ten years old. We need people to join the campaign to 'raise the age' and support calls for more resources and efforts to address the root-cause of why children are in the justice system so early in their lives.

Indigenous communities and experts have proven that programs that support children and their families when they are experiencing poverty, domestic violence and mental health issues are the most effective ways to reduce crime. Today's children, who are already disaffected by these social problems, need wrap-around support.

The juvenile justice statistics reflect a systemic problem rather than a problem with the children themselves. Indigenous children are not born with greater criminal intent. They are the victims of the policy inconsistencies and failures that have been mentioned throughout this book, such as the Northern Territory Intervention, the Community Development Program and Abbott's wrecking-ball budget in 2014.

Incarceration is not how a society helps troubled children and youth to get their lives on track, especially given that there are little to no services to help them while inside.

Find out more here: raisetheage.org.au

9   Combine your power – join an organisation

There are numerous organisations that individuals and groups can join, such as ANTAR, state and regional reconciliation groups, and unions. Union members can also join the First Nations Workers Alliance. A couple of great examples to look up are the Voice from the Heart Alliance and Allies for Uluru.

During the Voice campaign, some of the most effective organisations used the community alliance model. The Sydney Alliance, for example, brought together a wide range of organisations, such as religious groups, unions and multicultural societies.

We must put aside traditional differences and work together to achieve justice and recognition for First Peoples.

10   Record and share your truth

I invite you to record, and if you like, find ways to publish your stories if you supported the Yes campaign, or if you voted No and now think you would vote Yes if the opportunity arose again. You might do this by posting on social media on each anniversary, or by writing a memoir, a poem, or a letter to family. If you have the skills and profile, you may send an open letter or opinion piece to the local media. A quick internet search will give you some ideas about how to publish using these mediums. When you record the truth of what you experienced, you are documenting some important lessons for future generations of Australians. I encourage supporters to keep your photos as well. Share them proudly. You were there – on the right side of history.

11 *Recycle your Yes campaign merchandise*

In the same vein as above, I will share an idea about Yes campaign merchandise.

Immediately after the referendum, for several weeks, I felt a wave of sadness when I saw a Yes placard outside a house or sticker on a car. Then, after writing several articles about my feelings and thoughts about the future, and after catching up with some of the Elders who had been through such heartbreak before, I began to feel empowered when I saw the Yes symbol, rather than sad.

I think this says something about the power of the above action (10). Writing, recording, sharing and discussing your experiences can be healing. It is also an important stand we should take. Australians were not wrong to vote Yes. Nobody would have lost their property or privileges; our democracy would have become stronger – more complete; Indigenous Australians would have gained a fair-go and our nation's Constitution would have formally stated that our country has been 60,000 years in the making, not just 254. We should continue to express hope through displaying YES.

I dusted off my Yes shirt the day after my fishing trip with Will. I wore it, standing tall, my chin up, my eyes meeting strangers and with a smile on my face. Yes.

Use Yes merchandise as great a conversation starter – a tool to keep building the people-power side of the equation.

You may even give your merchandise an upgrade. Write why you voted Yes on your shirt. Or add the defiant words: 'Always Was, Always Will Be' above the big bold 'Yes'. Recycling your Yes merchandise is good for country!

All monies raised from the iron-on transfer and the merchandise will be donated to Indigenous causes.

12 Teach your children

We don't need to rely only on schools to educate our kids, parents and families can teach them too. Teach your children about Aboriginal and Torres Strait Islander culture and, in an age-appropriate way, the truth of Australia's colonial past.

Books are a wonderful way to educate children. From the traditional to the contemporary, Indigenous authors and illustrators are sharing their stories for you and your child to learn from together. You can reach other families this way as well. Books make the perfect gift for kids on their birthdays.

The best way to teach children is by setting an example for them to follow. At every opportunity, demonstrate your respect for Aboriginal and Torres Strait Islander Australia, your intolerance for racism, and let them see your efforts as you support the cause.

13 Make your vote count

When elections come around, you can find out which politicians have a good record in Indigenous Affairs and on broader, important social issues.

Find out what the candidate's record was during the referendum – did they actively support the Yes campaign? Do they have a strong, supportive position on topics such as universal healthcare and workers' rights, in addition to expressing their intention to listen to First Nations people and to act on their needs?

You can take this action further than your own vote, too. As I have discussed earlier, politics matters. So, I encourage you to share your reasons for supporting the candidate or the party you are voting for with your colleagues, family and friends.

Organisations acting

14 *Yes, this is part of your organisation's core business*

If your organisation is trying to decide whether gaining justice and recognition for the First Peoples of Australia is one of its responsibilities as a good corporate entity, the answer is absolutely yes. This is Aboriginal and Torres Strait Islander land and it was never ceded. Hence the saying, 'Always was, always will be'. It is our collective responsibility as Australians to make amends; it's our ethical mission, individually and collectively.

15 *Actively oppose racism*

All organisations in Australia should actively oppose racism. They should have an anti-racism policy that includes strict repercussions for an offence, and training for members and staff so they know what racism is. It is particularly important to educate staff and members about how racism is more than a matter of conscious personal behaviour; racism is perpetrated through unconscious bias, which includes people believing that racism is not a problem in this country because they have never experienced it. It is also systemic in how laws are made and enforced, and structural in how Indigenous peoples are subject to impactful decisions without having a genuine say.

16 *Appoint Indigenous experts to positions of leadership*

To achieve real change, it is important to appoint Indigenous people to positions at the highest levels of the organisational structure. This may be by appointing an Indigenous expert on your board, governing council, or executive team. That can be done in addition to having an internal or external Indigenous advisory council, and a direct relationship with Traditional Owners.

As well as bringing their professional expertise and experience to an organisation, Indigenous leaders possess a soft skill-set around engagement, lived experience as a minority, and cultural knowledge that should be valued.

To ensure there is a pipeline of talented Aboriginal and Torres Strait Islander professionals and leaders, investment in career pathways is vital too.

17 *Schools*

Principals, teachers, parents and carers, your school is so very important to justice and recognition. Second only to Indigenous communities, the next largest cohort of Australians who voted Yes was young people, thanks to you.

Curriculums already include Indigenous history and culture. To help weave First Peoples perspectives into all subjects and events, schools need resources.

Ngarrngga is the curriculum tool that I mentioned in chapter 10. It is an excellent collection of resources that are made by educators who understand what educators want, in collaboration with Indigenous knowledge experts.

Content created by Indigenous people in the arts may also be used across subjects. Traditional paintings can be used in geography, bush medicine in science, our stories in the stars and the way they were used to navigate in history, science and culture. Encourage teachers to use Indigenous knowledge in their lessons and visibly integrate Indigenous knowledge into your school's infrastructure.

The school initiatives I have enjoyed observing over the years are those that have been built on interactions with the local Indigenous community. It is especially significant and valuable to invite an Elder to regularly visit the students in their classrooms. Children will remember their interactions with Indigenous culture – the gentleness, generosity and wisdom – for the rest of their lives. Schools can create positive memories. Positive memories build resilience to negativity. Students will become part of the formula for a better future.

Finally, for schools to take actions such as those listed above, they need parents to actively support them. This may be done by participating in school parent councils, by volunteering and fundraising, and by respectfully encouraging teachers to bring our cultures into their lessons.

18 Universities

Some of Australia's universities have been around long enough to witness, and in some ways partake in, the acts of genocide against Aboriginal and Torres Strait Islander people. Now, they are often leaders in positive change.

An effective action is to continue to create scholarships for Aboriginal and Torres Strait Islander people who have aspirations in academia, and who would otherwise struggle to receive a tertiary education. It is important to ensure there is support for these students, including mentorship, culturally safe spaces, and inclusivity initiatives.

By now, all universities should have recognised their crucial role in truth-telling and justice. This may be through establishing a university-wide and public-facing truth-telling and justice project. For a university's commitment to be authentic, these initiatives would be in partnership with the communities they serve, and the best partnerships will be achieved when senior Indigenous leadership has been appointed in both academic and professional roles.

19 *Corporations*

I have discussed Reconciliation Action Plans (RAPs) and procurement policies in chapter 10. In summary here, they continue to be important, and all corporations should be on the RAP journey with Reconciliation Australia.

RAP commitments should be a business priority, adequately resourced, managed and staffed.

Consider how your organisation's RAP can provide the authorising environment required to join with important campaigns, such as 'Raise the Age'. After all, what is a commitment to reconciling our past, if we are not acting to help break the cycles that Indigenous youth are stuck in today?

Organisations can help create the conditions for members and employees to be part of the people power we need for justice and recognition. This should include creating an internal culture of inclusivity and understanding through cultural awareness courses and events. Contract First Nations educators to run talks and workshops; create community-mindedness by providing staff with volunteer days; and establish a library of First Nations literature in the workplace.

20 Unions

According to a *Guardian* Essential poll, two-thirds of people who were members of unions voted Yes,[1] the highest level of support compared with members of other organisations. With around 1.5 million members, the union movement will continue to be important to social justice in this country.

Effective actions that unions can take include educating members, delegates and officials, and negotiating clauses in agreements that support Indigenous workers. For example, enterprise agreements could provide remuneration to those workers who carry an additional cultural load in their employment. 'Cultural load' means the work that is asked of Indigenous workers, such as doing Acknowledgements of Country, answering questions or giving advice about Indigenous matters, and participating in committees and organising events, which are not part of their job. There could also be provisions that give recognition to Indigenous kinship structures…in bereavement leave, adoption leave and carers leave.

As recommended to all organisations, unions would be served well by ensuring that Indigenous members are in senior decision-making positions.

Good government policies

21 Politicians

It would be a great first step for politicians to listen to Aboriginal and Torres Strait Islander communities, act on their requests, and stop using their issues as a partisan matter.

22 *Political parties*

Political parties can be heartless machines. But at the end of the day, their policy platforms are decided by people.

People can become members of the political parties that align with their values. Use the democratic processes within the party to influence the policies they take to elections.

If the party has branch meetings in your area, you may want to engage at that level, inviting Indigenous advocates to inform members about local and national issues. These are forums that offer opportunities to bring about debate. You may come across resistance, but if you are prepared, you might change minds. You might cause the party to be better at representing the interests of Aboriginal and Torres Strait Islander people.

23 *Governments*

It is the role of government to establish a policy framework that understands the problems we are trying to solve. This means listening to the people who are most affected. What should follow is sensible policy that is able to be implemented on the ground and evaluated regularly with the flexibility to respond to changing needs.

Governments should play a supportive and resourcing role, with the community holding agency over the decisions on their Country.

When I talk about the good government policy factor in the formula above, I am not only talking about Indigenous Affairs policy. Broader good policy – social policies that improve the lot of all Australians, reversing the runaway wealth gap – is just as important. Good policy includes urgent action on climate change, as well as workers' rights, in a way that offers all working families a transition to new work without loss of pay or conditions.

People will struggle to hope that we can achieve justice and recognition for Indigenous Australians if they are struggling to have hope for their own futures.

Consistency

From time to time, we have had sufficient people power to advance Indigenous rights and our national understanding of the First Peoples. We have seen flashes of good government policy. And from corporations to unions, and across civil society, organisations have been stepping up to the crease to have a go.

But none of these factors has been consistent.

We won't see consistency without people power. We won't see consistency without organisations acting. We won't see consistency if governments continue to use Indigenous affairs as their go-to scapegoat.

Change starts with each of us.

This is the beginning, not the end.

Afterword

By the Monaghan family and their mum, Aunty Charney

Our mum, affectionately known as Charney to her loved ones, was born on the Clarence River near the pear tree that grew at Baryulgil. She was brought into the world by loving Bundjalung hands, in nature rather than within four walls, as her ancestors were before her.

Mum grew up in Baryulgil Square, which was a town established on a small patch of land that belonged to the Yulgilbar Pastoral Company, owned by the Hordern and Myer families. The arrangement was through a 99-year lease to the Aboriginal families of Daleys, Mundines and Gordons, so they could move from the riverbank huts.

Aboriginal children were barred from the mainstream school when Mum was a child because the white parents complained that they were dirty. So, the Aboriginal community campaigned to create their own school. After years of petitioning the New South Wales Government, an Aboriginal school was established, located near the asbestos mine dump site.

The asbestos mine near Baryulgil was the largest employer in the area. Ninety per cent of its workers were Black because Black people were cheap, and Black people were unlikely to be able to fight when the risk of asbestosis would eventually come to light. The company knew how dangerous their product was, yet they turned a blind eye as the community worked and played in the lethal dust. The tailings were used to make sandpits for the kids.

While Mum enjoyed some freedom, families at Baryulgil were still subject to the controlling Aboriginal Protection Board (APB). Education around culture and language was not allowed, and they lived in constant fear that the APB would steal the children.

At the age of fifteen, Mum was required to do domestic duties. She was sent to Sydney to work and live with white families to perform these tasks. After training she was sent to a station out west until she turned eighteen and moved to Nyngan, where she met our dad, Robert Snr.

Mixed marriages were frowned upon by the APB, so there was even more scrutiny of our family. Living back in the far west of New South Wales, daily visits from the APB officials weren't unusual at the Monaghan household. They constantly intimidated us. After Mum and Dad returned to Baryulgil with the first three of us kids, the APB was still present in our lives, but nothing would deter our parents. The Monaghan gang grew to five kids and our parents were now with other Aboriginal families that could provide support.

Mum loved life, and fishing was her favourite thing to do. She had her special spots along the river. She would have a bucket and bait ready when the kids got home from school.

She fished her whole life until she couldn't anymore, yet she still liked to drive to the riverside. The kids would throw a line in for her. Life on the river, waiting for a fish to bite, was her paradise. If she ran out of fishing worms, she would dig for more.

Mum had never voted. She told us that when she was a young woman working at the hospital in Nyngan, she went to vote for the first time, but was turned away by the white officials. This humiliated her so badly that she didn't try to vote again. But when we told her about the referendum for recognition and a Voice, she enrolled.

Mum had never forgotten the difficult times when racism was so much more on the surface. She wanted things to be different. She wanted to make sure her 'Yes' vote would be counted.

On 6 October, when some of us went with Mum to vote, a group of burly white men tried to intimidate us as we went to cast our votes at the pre-polls. Afterwards in the tavern as we had dinner, a man loudly stated that 'Abos get it all already'. In the hospital, it was openly alleged that a reason to vote No was because Indigenous people already 'get quicker service'.

The referendum brought us face to face with the racist views some hold. But it was them who were scared, not Mum.

Mum would not be deterred again.

She decorated her nursing home with Yes merchandise and spoke to the other residents about constitutional recognition. She turned the humiliation that she'd felt the first time she tried to vote into hope by writing an open letter (see below).

Listen to her gentle, generous way. Don't be saddened by her words and the rejection we felt on 14 October. Be emboldened, like her. Walk on past the naysayers. Keep saying, 'Yes.'

Mum passed away on 4 January 2024.

We love you, Mum. Your memory lives on.

ooooo

My name is Heather (Aunty Charney as known by my mob). I am a proud 84 yr old Aboriginal Bundjalung woman from the Clarence Valley, where I was born and have raised my 5 children.

I finally enrolled to vote in 2023. And I have Voted YES. And this is my story.

As a 21 yr old working and living in western NSW, I went to enrol to vote with a group of friends from work, and as we were lining up, I was pulled aside by an official and told 'You can't enrol, you are an "Aboriginee" and not allowed to vote.' A friend and later my husband (a NON-Indigenous man) stood by me and said, 'If you're not allowed to enrol and vote, then neither am I.' He stood by his word and never enrolled.

I voted YES because a YES vote is important because it recognises First Nations people, our history of this land, culture and contributions that we all have made to make Australia today.

There will be a platform where issues from the 'grass roots' up can be brought to the table and listened to. We will have a Voice that will last the generations and not be pulled out of the line because of 'politics of the day'.

I want there to be a positive change that can contribute to our communities and we be part of that contribution and change, that's why I enrolled and voted YES in 2023.

An invitation from Thomas

Aunty Charney and her family are an inspiration, along with many lovingly defiant Aboriginal and Torres Strait Islander families across this great country.

Dear reader, you are an inspiration with them. You have cared enough to listen; you have committed to take action; you are with us and we are millions in the Australian population – we who dare to hope.

I invite you now to use the roadmap in this book to keep walking toward justice and recognition for First Nations people. Take the lessons from the past to avoid the hazards along the way. Use the tools I and others can offer you to build bridges.

March on past those who will try to humiliate us.

Build a fire in your belly – never give up.

Useful resources

These lists of useful resources are by no means comprehensive. I hope that they will give you an overview of the wide and diverse range of First Nations resources, creations and creators, which you can build on.

Books

Pat Anderson AO and Mark Leibler AC, *Referendum Council Final Report*, 30 June 2017

Dean Ashenden, *Telling Tennant's Story: The strange career of the great Australian silence*, Black Inc., 2022

Bain Attwood and Andrew Markus, *Thinking Black*, Australian Institute of Aboriginal and Torres Strait Islander Studies, 2004

Bain Attwood and Andrew Markus, *The 1967 Referendum: Race, power and the Australian Constitution*, Aboriginal Studies Press, 2007

Lech Blain, *Quarterly Essay Issue 93, Bad Cop: Peter Dutton's strongman politics*, 18 March 2024

Claire G Coleman, *Lies Damn Lies: A personal exploration of the impact of colonisation*, Ultimo Press, 2021

Megan Davis & George Williams, *Everything you need to know about the Uluru Statement from the Heart*, UNSW Press, 2021

Pat Dodson and Julian Leeser, *Joint Select Committee on Constitutional Recognition Relating to Aboriginal and Torres Strait Islander Peoples Final Report*, 29 November 2018

Aaron Fa'aoso, *So Far, So Good: On connection, loss, laughter and the Torres Strait*, Pantera Press, 2022

Samantha Faulkner (anthology editor), *Growing up Torres Strait Islander in Australia*, Black Inc., 2024

First Knowledges series, Thames & Hudson Australia, 2021 onwards

Sean Flood, *Mabo: A symbol of struggle: the unfinished quest for Voice Treaty Truth*, Fink Consultancy, published 2018

Kevin Gilbert, *Because a White Man'll never do it*, Harper Collins Publishers, 1973

Stan Grant, *Australia Day*, Harper Collins Publishers, 2021

Stan Grant, *The Queen is Dead: The time has come for a reckoning*, Harper Collins Publishers, 2023

Jackie Huggins and Ngaire Jarro, *Jack of Hearts QX11594*, Magabala Books, 2022

Terri Janke, *True Tracks: Respecting Indigenous Knowledge and Culture*, NewSouth Publishing, 2021

Grace Karskens, *People of the River*, Allen & Unwin, Sydney, 2020

Rosalind Kidd, *Hard Labour, Stolen Wages: National Report on Stolen Wages*, Australians for Native Title and Reconciliation (ANTaR), 27 August 2007

JL Kohen, 'Pemulwuy (c1750–1802)', *Australian Dictionary of Biography*, supplementary volume, Melbourne University Press, Melbourne, 2005, pp 318–19

Marcia Langton, *Welcome to Country*, 2nd edition, Hardie Grant Explore, 2021

Marcia Langton, *The Welcome to Country Handbook: A Guide to Indigenous Australia*, Hardie Grant Explore, 2023

Marcia Langton and Tom Calma, *Indigenous Voice Co-Design Process – Final Report to the Australian Government*, July 2021

Robert Manne, 'Sorry Business', *The Monthly*, March 2008

David Marr, *Killing for Country: A Family Story*, Black Inc., 2023

Emeritus Professor John Maynard, *Fight for Liberty and Freedom*, AIATSIS, 2007

Thomas Mayo (editor & contributor), *Dear Son: Letters and Reflections from First Nations Fathers and Sons*, Hardie Grant Explore, 2021

Thomas Mayo, *Finding the Heart of the Nation: The journey of the Uluru Statement toward Voice, Treaty and Truth*, 2nd edition, Hardie Grant Explore, 2022

Thomas Mayo, Blak Douglas (illustrator), *Finding Our Heart: The story about the Uluru Statement for Young Australians*, Hardie Grant Explore, 2022

Thomas Mayo & Kerry O'Brien, Cathy Wilcox (illustrator), *The Voice to Parliament Handbook*, Hardie Grant Explore, 2023

Bernard Namok Jnr, Thomas Mayo, Tori-Jay Mordey, *Our Flag, Our Story: The Torres Strait Islander Flag*, Magabala Books, 2024

Ngarukuruwala Women's Group, *Murli La: Songs and Stories of the Tiwi Islands*, Hardie Grant Explore and the Indigenous Literacy Foundation, 2023

Bruce Pascoe, *Dark Emu*, Magabala Books, 2014

Noel Pearson, 'Declaration of Australia and the Australian People', Cape York Institute, 2 June 2018

Noel Pearson, *From the Heart: The 2022 Boyer Lectures*, YouTube

Cassandra Pybus, *A Very Secret Trade: The dark story of gentlemen collectors*, Allen and Unwin, 2024

Ziggy Ramo, *Human? A lie that has been killing us since 1788*, Pantera Press, 2024

Jonathan Richards, *The Secret War: A True History of Queensland's Native Police*, UQP, 2008

Archie Roach, *Tell Me Why*, Simon & Schuster, 2020

Archie Roach & Ruby Hunter, *Took the Children Away*, Simon & Schuster, 2020

Professor L Ryan, et al., 'Colonial Frontier Massacres in Australia, 1788–1930', The Centre for 21st Century Humanities, University of Newcastle, Stage 4.0, 2022, https://c21ch.newcastle.edu.au/colonialmassacres/

Rosie Smiler & Thomas Mayo, *Freedom Day: Vincent Lingiari and the story of the Wave Hill Walk-Off*, Hardie Grant Explore, 2021

WEH Stanner, *After the Dreaming: The 1968 Boyer Lectures*, Australian Broadcasting Commission, 1969

Victor Steffensen, *Fire Country: How Indigenous fire management could help save Australia*, Hardie Grant Books, 2020

Peter Stewart, *Demons at Dusk: Massacre at Myall Creek*, Temple House, 2007

Charlie Ward, *A Handful of Sand: The Gurindji Struggle, After the Walk-off*, Monash University Publishing, 2016

Eric Willmot, *Pemulwuy, the Rainbow Warrior*, Weldon, McMahons Point NSW, 1987

Clare Wright, *Naku Dharuk: The extraordinary story of how the people of Yirrkala changed the course of Australian democracy*, Text Publishing, 1 October 2024

Documentaries

Lousy Little Sixpence, dir. Gerald Bostock and Alec Morgan, 1983

First Australians, Blackfella Films, 2008

Croker Island Exodus, Tamarind Tree Pictures, 2012

In My Blood It Runs, Closer Productions, 2019

The Final Quarter, Shark Island Productions, 2019

Incarceration Nation, Bacon Factory Films/Bent 3 Land Productions/ NITV, 2021

Journey Home: David Gulpilil, Savage Films/Brindle Films, 2024

Films

Rabbit-Proof Fence, Rumbalara Films/The Australian Film Commission/AFFC, 2002

Samson and Delilah, CAAMA Productions/NSW Film and Television Office/Scarlett Pictures, 2009

Satellite Boy, Satellite Films/ABC, 2012

Charlie's Country, Adelaide Film Festival/Bula'bula Arts/Screen Australia, 2013

High Ground, Maxo Studios/Bunya Productions/Savage Films, 2020

The Drovers Wife, Bunya Productions/Oombarra Productions, 2022

TV series

Cleverman, ABC Australia/Goalpost Pictures, 2016–17

Mystery Road, Bunya Productions, 2018

Total Control, Blackfella Films/ABC Australia, 2019–24

Strait to the Plate, Lone Star Company, 2020
The Australian Wars, Blackfella Films, 2022
The First Inventors, NITV/NIAA/Ronde, 2023

Some First Nations bands, singers and songwriters

Here is a short list of recommendations, but there are many more artists I could name, and many of these artists move between genres.

Country: Troy Cassar-Daley, Roger Knox, Western Desert Band, David Williams, Blak Douglas, Adrian Burragubba, Ash Dargan, David Hudson, Glenn Skuthorpe

Rap: Briggs, Barkaa, Dobby, The Kid Laroi, Ziggy Ramo, J-Milla, JK-47, Mau Power, Say True God?

Pop: Baker Boy, Jessica Mauboy, Budjerah, Fred Leone, Electric Fields, Thelma Plum, Isaiah Firebrace, Mitch Tambo

Easy listening, blues, classical and reggae: Emma Donovan, Busby Marou, Chris Tamwoy, Joe Geia, Emily Wurramara, Saltwater Band, The Central Australian Aboriginal Women's Choir, Leah Flanagan, Lajamanu Teenage Band, Miiesha, B2M, William Barton,

Rock: King Stingray, Dan Sultan, Casey Donovan, East Journey, Black Arm Band, Scott Darlow

Some of the singers and bands that have lead the way: Kev Carmody, Yothu Yindi, Stiff Gins, NoK TuRNL, Dr G, Christine Anu, Shakaya

Back in the day: Warumpi Band, Coloured Stone, Mop and the Dropouts, Ruby Hunter, Archie Roach, No Fixed Address, Tiddas

Way back in the day: Jimmy Little, Seaman Dan, The Mills Sisters, Georgia Lee, The Sapphires, Col Hardy, Auriel Andrew, Isaac Yamma. Singer Fanny Cochrane Smith made the earliest recordings of traditional Tasmanian Aboriginal songs and language in 1899.

Festivals

Here are just some of the festivals you might want to go to:

DanceRites at the Sydney Opera House Forecourt each October, NSW, sydneyoperahouse.com/dancerites

Freedom Day Festival, Kalkarindji and Daguragu, NT, freedomday.com.au

Garma Festival of Traditional Cultures, Gulkula, NT, yyf.com.au/garma-festival

Garrmalang Festival, Darwin, NT, larrakia.com/garrmalang-festival

Laura Quinkan Dance Festival, Laura, Qld, lauraquinkanfestival.com.au

Winds of Zenadth Cultural Festival, Thursday Island, TSI/Qld, torres.qld.gov.au/community/winds-of-zendath-cultural-festival

Yabun Festival, Sydney, NSW, yabun.org.au

Yarrabah Music and Cultural Festival, Yarrabah, Qld, qmf.org.au/events/
yarrabah-festival

First Languages

The First Languages Australia website is an excellent resource.
Visit the General Interest page: firstlanguages.org.au/for-general-interest
The Gambay map and notes are also useful: gambay.com.au/teachers.

A few First Nations businesses

Here are some ways you can connect with Indigenous business and products:

Supply Nation has a database of verified Indigenous businesses. supplynation.org.au

Welcome to Country is a First Nations-led national not-for-profit organisation that connects Australians with Indigenous entrepreneurial products and experiences. welcometocountry.com

The Blak Markets are organised by First Hand Solutions Aboriginal Corporation in Sydney. It is a social enterprise, providing Indigenous artists, designers and small business owners with a place to showcase their wares, live and in person. blakmarkets.com.au

Wandu is dedicated to using and promoting Indigenous plants, foods and knowledge. warndu.com

Endnotes

Whether Yes or No, What's Next?

1   Western Australian Museum. (n.d.). *Breaking A Record – Making History.*
     Museum.wa.gov.au; Government of Western Australia. Retrieved April 4,
     2024, from https://museum.wa.gov.au/explore/online-exhibitions/1968-torres-
     strait-islander-track-laying-world-record/acknowledgement-c-2
2   Pearson, N. (2022, November 4). *Who we were, who we are, and who we can be.*
     Boyer Lectures. https://www.abc.net.au/listen/programs/boyerlectures/
     who-we-were-who-we-are-and-who-we-can-be/14095284

Hope

1   Australian Trade Union Institute. (2022, April 1). MUA: Here to stay! The
     1998 waterfront dispute. *Union History Blog.* https://atui.org.au/2022/04/01/
     mua-here-to-stay-the-1998-waterfront-dispute/
2   See, for example, *Andrew Cruickshank v Priceline Pty Ltd*, https://www6.austlii.
     edu.au/cgi-bin/viewdoc/au/other/AIRCSum/2007/292.html
3   Australian Indigenous Doctors' Association. (2021, August). *Growing the
     number of Aboriginal and Torres Strait Islander medical specialists – 2021:
     Self-assessments provided by specialist medical colleges against minimum and
     best-practice standards aimed at attracting, recruiting and retaining Aboriginal and
     Torres Strait Islander specialist trainees.* Australian Indigenous Doctors'
     Association, Canberra. https://aida.org.au/app/uploads/2022/03/
     AIDA-Growing-medical-specialists-report-2021_v2.pdf

What about the Uluṟu Statement from the Heart now?

1   Yes23. (2017, May 26). *Uluṟu Statement from the Heart.* Yes23.
     https://www.yes23.com.au/uluru_statement

Always Was – The first 65,000 years

1   Hamilton, C. (2015, October 15). The Price of God at Coronation Hill. *The
     Conversation.*
     https://theconversation.com/the-price-of-god-at-coronation-hill-49235
2   Cook, J., Hutchinson, J., Wallis, S., & Bolckow, H.W.F. (1768). *Journal of
     H.M.S.* Endeavour. Retrieved March 12, 2024, from
     http://nla.gov.au/nla.obj-228958440
3   Laurie, V. (2023, July 21). The 50,000-year-old "drop-in centre" that was nearly
     demolished, Good Weekend, *Sydney Morning Herald.*
4   Cooper, D. (2016, November 3). Oldest known evidence of Aboriginal

settlement in arid Australia found in Flinders Ranges rock shelter. *ABC Science.*
https://www.abc.net.au/news/science/2016-11-03/
rock-shelter-shows-early-aboriginal-settlement-in-arid-australia/7983864

5   Hamm, G., Mitchell, P., Arnold, L. J., Prideaux, G. J., Questiaux, D., Spooner,
N. A., Levchenko, V. A., Foley, E. C., Worthy, T. H., Stephenson, B., Coulthard,
V., Coulthard, C., Wilton, S., & Johnston, D. (2016). Cultural innovation and
megafauna interaction in the early settlement of arid Australia. *Nature,*
539(7628), 280–283. https://doi.org/10.1038/nature20125

6   Cooper, D. (2016, November 3). Oldest known evidence of Aboriginal
settlement in arid Australia found in Flinders Ranges rock shelter. *ABC Science.*

7   Clarkson, C., Jacobs, Z., Marwick, B., Fullagar, R., Wallis, L., Smith, M.,
Roberts, R. G., Hayes, E., Lowe, K., Carah, X., Florin, S. A., McNeil, J., Cox,
D., Arnold, L. J., Hua, Q., Huntley, J., Brand, H. E. A., Manne, T., Fairbairn,
A., & Shulmeister, J. (2017). Human occupation of northern Australia by
65,000 years ago. *Nature,* 547(7663), 306–310. https://doi.org/10.1038/
nature22968

8   Weule, G., & James, F. (2017, July 20). Indigenous rock shelter in Top End
pushes Australia's human history back to 65,000 years. *ABC Science/ABC*
Darwin. https://www.abc.net.au/news/science/2017-07-20/
aboriginal-shelter-pushes-human-history-back-to-65,000-years/8719314

9   First Languages Australia & Commonwealth of Australia. (2023). *Voices of*
Country – Australia's Action Plan for the International Decade of Indigenous
Languages. https://www.arts.gov.au/publications/
voices-country-australias-action-plan-international-decade-indigenous-
languages-2022-2032

10   Gambay – First Languages Australia. (n.d.). *Gambay – First Languages Map.*
Retrieved March 12, 2024, from https://gambay.com.au/languages

11   Aboriginal and Torres Strait Islander Social Justice Commissioner. (2011).
Chapter 2: Lateral violence in Aboriginal and Torres Strait Islander
communities. In *Social Justice Report 2011* (pp. 50–98). Australian Human
Rights Commission. www.humanrights.gov.au/social_justice/sj_report/
sjreport11/index.html

12   ANTaR Victoria, used with permission of Dr Yunupingu's brother, Djawa, and
the Yunupingu family. (n.d.). *A National Makarrata.* ANTaR Victoria.
Retrieved March 12, 2024, from https://antarvictoria.org.
au/a-national-marrata

Always Will Be – A long history of injustice

1   Committee on Returns of Felons, 1 April 1779, *Journals of the House of*
Commons (London: House of Commons, 1779), quoted in McBride, L. &
Smith, M. (2021). 'Plans for a colony', Australian Museum.

https://australian.museum/learn/first-nations/unsettled/recognising-invasions/plans-for-a-colony/

2　For information about Arabanoo, see Smith, K. V. (2010). *Arabanoo, The Dictionary of Sydney*. https://dictionaryofsydney.org/entry/arabanoo

3　Smith, K. V. (2010). *Arabanoo, The Dictionary of Sydney*. https://dictionaryofsydney.org/entry/arabanoo

4　Greer, G. (2003). *Quarterly Essay 11 Whitefella Jump Up: The Shortest Way to Nationhood*. Black Inc. Books. https://kooriweb.org/foley/resources/pdfs/143.pdf

5　As told in a damagingly racist recount of the colonisers' stories of the time: Bonwick, J. (1856). *William Buckley: the wild white man, and his Port Phillip black friends*. Goodall & Demaine, Printers.

6　For information about Bennelong, see Smith, K. V. (2013). *Woollarawarre Bennelong, The Dictionary of Sydney*. https://dictionaryofsydney.org/entry/woollarawarre_bennelong

7　Baudin, N., Bonnemains, J., Argentin, J.-M., & Marin, M. (2000). *Mon voyage aux terres australes*. Imprimerie Nationale.

8　Banks, S. J. (1790). Series 37.12: Letter received by Banks from Arthur Phillip, 26 July 1790. *State Library of NSW Catalogue, Sir Joseph Banks Papers, 1767–1822*. SAFE/Banks Papers/Series 37.12. https://archival.sl.nsw.gov.au/Details/archive/110579208

9　Becke, L., & Jeffery, W. (1899). *Admiral Phillip: the founding of New South Wales*. T. F. Unwin.

10　Tench, W. (1961). *Sydney's First Four Years: being a reprint of A narrative of the expedition to Botany Bay and A complete account of the settlement at Port Jackson*. Angus and Robertson, Royal Australian Historical Society. (Original work published 1793) with an introduction and annotations by L.F. Fitzhardinge.

11　Tench, W. (1961). *Sydney's First Four Years: being a reprint of A narrative of the expedition to Botany Bay and A complete account of the settlement at Port Jackson*. Angus and Robertson, Royal Australian Historical Society.

12　Easty, J. (1973). Memorandum of the Transactions of a Voyage from England to Botany Bay, 1787-1793. *State Library of NSW Catalogue*. https://www.sl.nsw.gov.au/collection-items/john-easty-journal-1786-1793-titled-pt-jno-easty-memorandum-transa-voiage-sic

13　Sahni, N. (2020). *Aboriginal Resistance Leader - Pemulwuy, Parramatta History and Heritage*. City of Parramatta. https://historyandheritage.cityofparramatta.nsw.gov.au/research-topics/aboriginal/aboriginal-resistance-leader-pemulwuy

14　National Museum of Australia. (2009). *Pemulwuy, 1792: Aboriginal warrior Pemulwuy leads resistance against Sydney colonists*. Defining Moments, National Museum of Australia. https://www.nma.gov.au/defining-moments/resources/pemulwuy

15   For more information about Pemulwuy, see Smith, K. V. (2010). *Pemulwuy, The Dictionary of Sydney*. https://dictionaryofsydney.org/entry/pemulwuy

16   Pedersen, H., & Woorunmurra, B. (2011). *Jandamarra and the Bunuba resistance*. Magabala Books. (Original work published 1995)

17   Pybus, C. (2020). *Truganini: journey through the apocalypse*. Allen & Unwin.

18   Connors, L. (2015). *Warrior : a legendary leader's dramatic life and violent death on the colonial frontier*. Allen & Unwin.

19   Idriess, I. (1933). *Drums of Mer*. Angus and Robertson.

20   Matson-Green, V. maikutena. (2006). *Walyer*. The Companion to Tasmanian History; Centre for Tasmanian Historical Studies. https://www.utas.edu.au/library/companion_to_tasmanian_history/W/Walyer.htm

21   South West Aboriginal Land & Sea Council. (2010). *Yagan*. Kaartdijin Noongar, Noongar Knowledge. https://www.noongarculture.org.au/yagan/

22   Perkins, R. (2022). *The Australian Wars*. ABC. https://www.sbs.com.au/ondemand/tv-series/the-australian-wars

23   Ryan, L., Debenham, J., Pascoe, B., Smith, R., Owen, C., Richards, J., Gilbert, S., Anders, R. J., Usher, K., Price, D., Newley, J., Brown, M., Le, L. H., & Fairbairn, H. (2022). *Colonial Frontier Massacres in Australia, 1788–1930*. Centre for 21st Century Humanities, University of Newcastle. https://c21ch.newcastle.edu.au/colonialmassacres/

24   *The killing times: a massacre map of Australia's frontier wars*. (2022, March 16). *The Guardian*. https://www.theguardian.com/australia-news/ng-interactive/2019/mar/04/massacre-map-australia-the-killing-times-frontier-wars

25   *New evidence reveals Aboriginal massacres committed on extensive scale*. (2022, March 16). University of Newcastle, University News. https://www.newcastle.edu.au/newsroom/featured/new-evidence-reveals-aboriginal-massacres-committed-on-extensive-scale

26   Medcalf, R. (1993, April 7). Flour laced with arsenic brings on mass poisoning. *Koori Mail*. https://aiatsis.gov.au/collection/featured-collections/koori-mail Issue 48, from the series 'Rivers of Blood', originally published in the *Northern Star*, Lismore

27   FitzSimons, P. (2023, June 9). Myall Creek apology, I've told many tales of tragedy, but never one as haunting as this. *The Sydney Morning Herald*. https://www.smh.com.au/national/nsw/myall-creek-apology-20230608-p5dexz.html

28   Stewart, P. (2007). *Demons at dusk: massacre at Myall Creek*. Temple House.

29   Allam, L. (2018, August 24). Coniston massacre descendants reunite to push for national truth-telling process. *The Guardian*. https://www.theguardian.com/australia-news/2018/aug/24/coniston-massacre-descendants-reunite-to-push-for-national-truth-telling-process

Becoming Australia

1 Barton, E. (1898). *Official Report of the National Australasian Convention Debates (Third Session)*. pp.228–229. Parliament of Australia. https://parlinfo.aph.gov.au/parlInfo/search/display/display.w3p;query=Id%3A%22constitution%2Fconventions%2F1898-1096%22

2 For a discussion of how this phrase was used to justify protectionism policies from 1870 onwards, see Carter, J. (1998). *REPLY: Smoothing the Dying Pillow*. H-Net Discussion Networks | Humanities and Social Sciences Online. https://lists.h-net.org/cgi-bin/logbrowse.pl?trx=vx&list=h-anzau&month=9801&week=b&msg=6C6XT8j04zXGWrpNnAysdA&user=&pw=

3 Deakin, A. (2019). *From our special correspondent: Alfred Deakin's letters to the London Morning Post* (Vol. 1). Australian Parliamentary Library. https://nla.gov.au/nla.obj-3008931127/view (Original work published 1901)

4 Harold Finch-Hatton in 1886 quoted in Evans, R., Saunders, K., & Cronin, K. (1988). *Race Relations in Colonial Queensland: A History of Exclusion, Exploitation and Extermination*. University of Queensland Press. https://espace.library.uq.edu.au/view/UQ:203580

5 Ward, C. (2016). *A handful of sand: the Gurindji struggle, after the walk-off*. Monash University Publishing.

6 Abbott, T. (2020, August 5). Episode 2: Australia's Future (J. Roskam, Interviewer) [Interview]. In *Institute of Public Affairs*. https://ipa.org.au/publications-ipa/opinion/tony-abbott-john-interview-episode-2

7 Murphy, K. (2020, June 12). Scott Morrison sorry for 'no slavery in Australia' claim and acknowledges 'hideous practices'. *The Guardian*. https://www.theguardian.com/australia-news/2020/jun/12/scott-morrison-sorry-for-no-slavery-in-australia-claim-and-acknowledges-hideous-practices

8 *Bringing Them Home* Report. (2009). *Historical Context - The Stolen Generations*. Humanrights.gov.au. https://bth.humanrights.gov.au/significance/historical-context-the-stolen-generations

9 Manne, R. (2008, March 5). Sorry business: The road to the apology. *The Monthly*. https://www.themonthly.com.au/monthly-essays-robert-manne-sorry-business-road-apology-823#mtr

10 Australian Human Rights Commission 2017. (1997). *Bringing Them Home: National Inquiry into the Separation of Aboriginal and Torres Strait Islander Children from Their Families*. https://humanrights.gov.au/sites/default/files/content/pdf/social_justice/bringing_them_home_report.pdf

11 Australian Human Rights Commission 2017. (1997). *Bringing Them Home: National Inquiry into the Separation of Aboriginal and Torres Strait Islander Children from Their Families*.

12   To hear John Howard talking about the National Apology, see Krishnan, S. (2022, January 1). *John Howard has criticised Kevin Rudd's 2008 apology to the Stolen Generations.* SBS News. https://www.sbs.com.au/news/article/john-howard-has-criticised-kevin-rudds-2008-apology-to-the-stolen-generations/47t04w7ca

13   Rudd, K. (2018, February 9). *Apology to Australia's Indigenous peoples (2008)* [ABC News In-depth | Youtube]. https://youtu.be/RThkO3XBThs?si=V3SKOvtJlicNLk-c

14   Parliament of Australia. (2008, February 13). *Apology to Australia's Indigenous Peoples.* Parliament of Australia website. https://www.aph.gov.au/Visit_Parliament/Art/Icons/Apology_to_Australias_Indigenous_Peoples

15   Parliament of Australia. (2008, February 13). *Apology to Australia's Indigenous Peoples.* Parliament of Australia website.

16   Butler, J. (2023, February 13). Dutton apologises for boycotting Rudd's apology to stolen generations. *The Guardian.* https://www.theguardian.com/australia-news/2023/feb/13/dutton-apologises-for-boycotting-rudds-apology-to-stolen-generations

17   Butler, J. (2023, February 13). Dutton apologises for boycotting Rudd's apology to stolen generations.

18   Commonwealth of Australia. (2023, June 22). *Parliamentary Debates.* House of Representatives. [ParlInfo]. https://parlinfo.aph.gov.au/parlInfo/download/chamber/hansardr/26709/toc_pdf/House%20of%20Representatives_2023_06_22_Official.pdf

19   SNAICC – National Voice for our Children. (2023, November 29). *Aboriginal and Torres Strait Islander children and families paying the price for government inaction, report finds.* SNAICC – National Voice for Our Children website. https://www.snaicc.org.au/aboriginal-and-torres-strait-islander-children-and-families-paying-the-price-for-government-inaction-report-finds/

20   Australian Institute of Health and Welfare. (2023). *Suicide & Indigenous Australians.* Australian Institute of Health and Welfare; Australian Government. https://www.aihw.gov.au/suicide-self-harm-monitoring/data/populations-age-groups/suicide-indigenous-australians

21   Sargeant, C. (2018, January 26). *The many different dates we've celebrated Australia Day.* SBS Voices. https://www.sbs.com.au/voices/article/the-many-different-dates-weve-celebrated-australia-day/vuhb3ar1c

22   National Museum of Australia. (2023). *Wave Hill Walk-Off.* Defining Moments, National Museum of Australia. https://www.nma.gov.au/defining-moments/resources/wave-hill-walk-off

23   See: Matthew Thomas, 'The 1967 Referendum', Parliament of Australia website, 25 May 2017, www.aph.gov.au/About_Parliament/

Parliamentary_Departments/Parliamentary_Library/FlagPost/2017/May/
The_1967_Referendum

24   See: National Museum of Australia. (1972). *Aboriginal Tent Embassy*. Defining
Moments, National Museum of Australia. www.nma.gov.au/defining-
moments/resources/aboriginal-tent-embassy

25   Whitlam, G. (1972, November 13). *It's Time: Gough Whitlam's 1972 Election
Policy Speech* [Australianpolitics.com]. https://australianpolitics.
com/1972/11/13/whitlam-1972-election-policy-speech.html

26   See the photo of Vincent Lingiari and Gough Whitlam at https://www.
portrait.gov.au/magazines/24/a-handful-of-sand

27   For the full Redfern Speech, see Keating, P. (1992, December 10). *Australian
Launch of the International Year for the World's Indigenous People (The Redfern
Speech)* [Transcript]. https://pmtranscripts.pmc.gov.au/sites/default/files/
original/00008765.pdf

28   Aboriginal and Torres Strait Islander Social Justice Commissioner. (2009).
Native Title Report 2008 (Appendix 3: Social Justice Package –
recommendations made in 1995). Australian Human Rights Commission
2009. https://humanrights.gov.au/sites/default/files/content/social_justice/
nt_report/ntreport08/pdf/appendix3.pdf

29   Remeikis, A., & Butler, J. (2023, October 12). Voice referendum: factchecking
the seven biggest pieces of misinformation pushed by the no side. *The
Guardian*. https://www.theguardian.com/australia-news/2023/oct/12/
indigenous-voice-to-parliament-referendum-misinformation-fact-checked

30   Haughton, J. (2023, June 16). *Former Aboriginal and Torres Strait Islander
Australian Government representative and advisory bodies: a quick guide*.
Parliament of Australia. https://www.aph.gov.au/About_Parliament/
Parliamentary_departments/Parliamentary_Library/pubs/rp/rp2223/Quick_
Guides/FormerAboriginalandTorresStraightIslanderRepresentativeBodies

31   Fitzpatrick, S. (2018, August 1). Dismantling ATSIC probably a mistake, says
Amanda Vanstone. *The Australian*. https://www.theaustralian.com.au/nation/
dismantling-atsic-probably-a-mistake-says-amanda-vanstone/news-story/8637
b58bd217f610b71477f83cbdd90a

32   James, F. (2022, July 24). Residents who lived through the NT intervention
plead for governments to "listen", 15 years on. *ABC News*. https://www.abc.net.
au/news/2022-07-24/nt-intervention-reflections-15-years-on/101238592

33   Australian Human Rights Commission. (2011, November 2). *The Suspension
and Reinstatement of the RDA and Special Measures in the NTER* . Humanrights.
gov.au. https://humanrights.gov.au/our-work/race-discrimination/publications/
suspension-and-reinstatement-rda-and-special-measures

34   Castan Centre for Human Rights Law. (n.d.). *What is the Northern Territory*

Intervention? Monash University. https://www.monash.edu/law/research/centres/castancentre/research-areas/indigenous/the-northern-territory-intervention/the-northern-territory-intervention-an-evaluation/what-is-the-northern-territory-intervention

35   Maguire, G. (2017, June 26). The NT "Intervention" led to some changes in Indigenous health, but the social cost may not have been worth it. *The Conversation.* https://theconversation.com/the-nt-intervention-led-to-some-changes-in-indigenous-health-but-the-social-cost-may-not-have-been-worth-it-78833

36   O'Mara, P. (2010). Health impacts of the Northern Territory intervention. *Medical Journal of Australia, 192*(10), 546–548. https://doi.org/10.5694/j.1326-5377.2010.tb03631.x

37   Tomevska, S. (2023, October 22). *Why are calls for a royal commission into child sexual abuse causing a stir?* SBS News. https://www.sbs.com.au/news/article/why-are-calls-for-a-royal-commission-into-child-sexual-abuse-causing-a-stir/dcylgg2o1

Leaners and lifters

1   Daley, P. (2014, November 27). Abbott's homogeneous approach to Indigenous affairs will not erase the stain on Australia's soul. *The Guardian.* https://www.theguardian.com/commentisfree/2014/nov/27/abbotts-homogenous-approach-to-indigenous-affairs-will-not-erase-the-stain-on-australias-soul

2   Whiteford, P. (2023, July 23). The welfare myth of "lifters" and "leaners" must be put behind us so robodebt is never repeated. *The Guardian.* https://www.theguardian.com/commentisfree/2023/jul/23/the-welfare-myth-of-lifters-and-leaners-must-be-put-behind-us-so-robodebt-is-never-repeated

3   The Commonwealth of Australia. (2014). *Budget 2014–15 | Budget Paper No.2* (p. 185). Commonwealth of Australia 2014. https://archive.budget.gov.au/2014-15/bp2/BP2_consolidated.pdf

4   Australian Bureau of Statistics. (2020-2022). *Aboriginal and Torres Strait Islander life expectancy.* ABS. https://www.abs.gov.au/statistics/people/aboriginal-and-torres-strait-islander-peoples/aboriginal-and-torres-strait-islander-life-expectancy/latest-release

5   Commonwealth of Australia. (2014). *Budget 2014–15 | Budget Paper No.2* (p. 185). Commonwealth of Australia 2014.

6   Dunlop, G. (2018, November 22). *Scullion defends giving Indigenous funds to cattle and fishing lobbies.* NITV; SBS. https://www.sbs.com.au/nitv/article/scullion-defends-giving-indigenous-funds-to-cattle-and-fishing-lobbies/9b6catr13

7   Dunlop, G. (2018, November 22). *Scullion defends giving Indigenous funds to cattle and fishing lobbies.* NITV; SBS.

8   Australian National Audit Office. (2017). Auditor-General Report No.35 of
         2016–17 | Indigenous Advancement Strategy. In *ANAO.gov.au*.
         Commonwealth of Australia 2017. https://www.anao.gov.au/work/
         performance-audit/indigenous-advancement-strategy

9   Jordan, K. (2015). Inquiry into Economic Development in Aboriginal
         Communities. In *NSW Parliament*. Centre for Aboriginal Economic Policy
         Research | Australian National University. https://www.parliament.nsw.gov.au/
         lcdocs/submissions/52460/008%20Dr%20Kirrily%20Jordan.pdf

10   Altman, J. (2016, December 16). *Making a living differently*. Inside Story.
         https://insidestory.org.au/making-a-living-differently

11   Altman, J. (2016, December 16). *Making a living differently*. Inside Story.

12   Australian Council of Trade Unions. (2018, May 2). *Racist remote welfare
         program failing on every measure: new report*. Australian Council of Trade
         Unions. https://www.actu.org.au/media-release/racist-remote-welfare-
         program-failing-on-every-measure-new-report/

13   Altman, J. (2016, December 16). *Making a living differently*. Inside Story.

14   Browne, B. (2021, May 13). *Welcome End to So-Called "Community Development
         Program" (CDP)*. The Australia Institute. https://australiainstitute.org.au/post/
         welcome-end-to-so-called-community-development-program-cdp/

15   Australian Institute of Health and Welfare. (2020). *Aboriginal and Torres Strait
         Islander Health Performance Framework 2020 summary report. Cat. no. IHPF 2*.
         AIHW. https://www.indigenoushpf.gov.au/getattachment/65fbaaf3-100c-
         4df5-941c-a8455922693c/2020-summary-ihpf-2.pdf

16   Medhora, S. (2015, March 10). Remote communities are "lifestyle choices",
         says Tony Abbott. *The Guardian*. https://www.theguardian.com/australia-
         news/2015/mar/10/
         remote-communities-are-lifestyle-choices-says-tony-abbott

17   Prime Minister and Cabinet. (2016, March 18). *Indigenous Rangers Program*.
         National Indigenous Australians Agency. https://www.niaa.gov.au/indigenous-
         affairs/environment/indigenous-rangers-program

18   Ikonomou, T. (2022, June 22). Indigenous people facing "economic apartheid",
         policy shift needed. *National Indigenous Times*. https://nit.com.au/22-06-2022/
         3311/indigenous-people-facings-economic-apartheid-policy-shift-needed

19   Northern Land Council. (2022, February 25). *History made with Aboriginal Sea
         Company incorporation*. Northern Land Council. https://www.nlc.org.au/
         media-publications/history-made-with-aboriginal-sea-company-incorporation

20   Commonwealth of Australia 2021. (2017). *Final Report of the Referendum
         Council | Appendix G - Kirribilli Statement*. Referendum Council.

21   Commonwealth of Australia 2021. (2017). *Final Report of the Referendum
         Council | Appendix G - Kirribilli Statement*. Referendum Council.

22   Albanese, A. (2022, May 22). *Anthony Albanese's Prime Minister acceptance speech*

[Transcript]. https://www.abc.net.au/news/2022-05-22/
anthony-albanese-acceptance-speech-full-transcript/101088736

Understanding what we are up against

1   Butler, J. (2023, December 22). Makarrata commission in limbo after failure of Indigenous voice referendum. *The Guardian*. https://www.theguardian.com/australia-news/2023/dec/22/makarrata-commission-in-limbo-after-failure-of-indigenous-voice-referendum

2   Rintoul, C. (2024, January 8). Australian councils ditch welcome-to-country ceremonies, cultural gestures in droves post-Voice defeat. *The West Australian*.

3   Morgan, T. (2024, March 12). Federal, NT governments announces 10-year, $4 billion remote housing agreement. *ABC News*. https://www.abc.net.au/news/2024-03-12/10-year-nt-remote-housing-agreement-worth-4-billion-announcement/103574262

4   O'Connor, B., Burney, L., & Scrymgour, M. (2024, February 14). $30 million to deliver remote training hubs to First Nations peoples in Central Australia. *Ministers' Media Centre*. https://ministers.dewr.gov.au/oconnor/30-million-deliver-remote-training-hubs-first-nations-peoples-central-australia

5   Wallace, R., Knipe, S., & Woodroffe, T. (2024, March 15). There's an extra $1 billion on the table for NT schools. This could change lives if spent well. *The Conversation*. https://theconversation.com/theres-an-extra-1-billion-on-the-table-for-nt-schools-this-could-change-lives-if-spent-well-225678

6   See the Uluru Statement from the Heart in chapter 2.

7   Stanner, WEH. (1968). *After the dreaming*. Boyer Lectures. Published by Australian Broadcasting Commission; Sydney, 1972.

8   Pearson, N. (2022, November 4). *Who we were, who we are, and who we can be*. Boyer Lectures. https://www.abc.net.au/listen/programs/boyerlectures/who-we-were-who-we-are-and-who-we-can-be/14095284

Flooding the zone with truth and hope

1   Stengel, R. (2020, June 26). We Should Be as Worried About Domestic Disinformation as We Are About International Campaigns. *Time*. https://time.com/5860215/domestic-disinformation-growing-menace-america/

2   Remeikis, A., & Butler, J. (2023, October 12). Voice referendum: factchecking the seven biggest pieces of misinformation pushed by the no side. *The Guardian*. https://www.theguardian.com/australia-news/2023/oct/12/indigenous-voice-to-parliament-referendum-misinformation-fact-checked

3   abcqanda. (2016). Social Determinants of Health - Q&A | 29 August 2016 [YouTube video]. In *ABC Q+A*. https://www.youtube.com/watch?v=WbD4x2jCWyg

4   Abbott, T. (2023, July 24). "Power grab by activists!": Tony Abbott blasts Indigenous Voice (B. Fordham, Interviewer) [Interview]. In *2GB Sydney*.

https://www.2gb.compower-grab-by-activists-tony-abbott-blasts-
indigenous-voice/

5   Biddle, N. (2019, January 14). FactCheck Q&A: is $30 billion spent every year
    on 500,000 Indigenous people in Australia? *The Conversation*. https://
    theconversation.com/factcheck-qanda-is-30-billion-spent-every-year-on-
    500-000-indigenous-people-in-australia-64658

6   Campbell, D. (2023, August 4). Tony Abbott is wrong – the NIAA doesn't
    spend $30 billion a year on Indigenous programs. *RMIT University News*.
    https://www.rmit.edu.au/news/factlab-meta/niaa-does-not-spend-$30b-on-
    indigenous-programs-annually

7   Biddle, N. (2019, January 14). FactCheck Q&A: is $30 billion spent every year
    on 500,000 Indigenous people in Australia? *The Conversation*.

8   Australian Institute of Aboriginal and Torres Strait Islander Studies. (2021,
    September 11). *Proof of Aboriginality*. AIATSIS. https://aiatsis.gov.au/
    proof-aboriginality

9   Australian Human Rights Commission. (2022). *What Is Racism?* Australian
    Human Rights Commission. https://humanrights.gov.au/our-work/race-
    discrimination/what-racism

10 Rose, T., & Basford Canales, S. (2023, September 15). Indigenous people
    "disgusted" by Jacinta Nampijinpa Price's "simply wrong" comments on
    colonisation, Burney says. *The Guardian*. https://www.theguardian.com/
    australia-news/2023/sep/15/jacinta-nampijinpa-price-comments-colonisation-voice-
    referendum-linda-burney

11 Moggridge, B., Beal, C., Lansbury, N., University of Queensland & University
    of Canberra. (2022, November 16). *Countless reports show water is undrinkable in
    many Indigenous communities. Why has nothing changed?* Public-Health.uq.edu.
    au; UQ School of Public Health. https://public-health.uq.edu.au/
    article/2022/11/countless-reports-show-water-undrinkable-many-indigenous-
    communities-why-has-nothing-changed

12 Wyrwoll, P. R., Manero, A., Taylor, K. S., Rose, E. & Quentin Grafton, R.
    (2022). Measuring the gaps in drinking water quality and policy across regional
    and remote Australia. *npj Clean Water*, 5(1), 1–14. https://doi.org/10.1038/
    s41545-022-00174-1

13 Al-Yaman, F. (2017). The Australian Burden of Disease Study: impact and
    causes of illness and death in Aboriginal and Torres Strait Islander people,
    2011. *Public Health Research & Practice*, 27(4). https://doi.org/10.17061/
    phrp2741732

14 Australian Medical Association. (2020). AMA submission to the inquiry into
    food prices and food security in remote Indigenous communities. In *Parliament
    of Australia*. Australian Medical Association.

15   Fitzgerald, R. (2022, June 25). Remote Northern Territory food prices skyrocket, worries for health of communities. *ABC News/ABC Katherine*. https://www.abc.net.au/news/2022-06-25/food-prices-in-remote-northern-territory-communities-skyrocket/101160112

16   Richardson, H., André, J., & Testa, C. (2023, June 30). Health services failed in care for three Doomadgee women who died of rheumatic heart disease. *ABC News/ABC Far North*. https://www.abc.net.au/news/2023-06-30/coroner-hands-down-doomadgee-rhd-inquest-findings/102545514

17   Cassidy, C. (2024, February 25). Lowering cost of higher education critical to meeting Australia's skills shortage, report warns. *The Guardian*. https://www.theguardian.com/australia-news/2024/feb/25/lowering-cost-of-higher-education-critical-to-meeting-australias-skills-shortage-report-warns

18   Taylor, J. (2022, December 20). Indigenous deaths in custody rises to 516 since the 1991 royal commission, report says. *The Guardian*. https://www.theguardian.com/australia-news/2022/dec/20/indigenous-deaths-in-custody-rises-to-516-since-the-1991-royal-commission-report-says

19   RMIT ABC Fact Check. (2019, October 10). Linda Burney says Australia is the only first world nation with a colonial history that doesn't recognise its first people in its constitution. Is she correct? *ABC News*. https://www.abc.net.au/news/2019-10-10/fact-check3a-is-australia-the-only-first-world-nation-with-a-c/11583706

A guide to protocol, awareness and respect

1   Davis, M. (2020, July 1). Reconciliation and the promise of an Australian homecoming. *The Monthly*, July 2020. https://www.themonthly.com.au/issue/2020/july/megan-davis/reconciliation-and-promise-australian-homecoming#mtr

2   *Racial Discrimination Act 1975* (Cth), s 18C. https://www5.austlii.edu.au/au/legis/cth/consol_act/rda1975202/s18c.html

Overcoming uncertainty and fear with familiarity

1   Australian Institute of Aboriginal and Torres Strait Islander Studies. (2020). *Core cultural learning*. AIATSIS. https://aiatsis.gov.au/about/what-we-do/core-cultural-learning

What's next – Starting today

1   Lewis, P. (2023, October 17). The voices of division will keep winning unless we learn these hard lessons from the referendum. *The Guardian*. https://www.theguardian.com/australia-news/commentisfree/2023/oct/17/the-voices-of-division-will-keep-winning-unless-we-learn-these-hard-lessons-from-the-referendum

Acknowledgements

My deepest thanks to my wife, Mel, and kids, Shayla, Tiah, Celestino, William and Ruby; my mum and dad, wider family in the Torres Strait, the union movement, and the Larrakia Traditional Owners where I live in Darwin. They are the sources of my hope.

I appreciate Bernadette Foley, a good comrade, guide and editor of this and many of my books. Hardie Grant has been a brilliant publisher. Thank you, Sandy Grant, Fiona Hardie, Roxy Ryan, Astrid Browne, Amanda Louey and freelance editor Rosanna Dutson. Many thanks to my agent Clare Forster.

Putting this book together in only several months required the best assistance possible. I thank Jade Ritchie for helping me with the 'Guide to protocol, awareness and respect' chapter; Patrycja Slawuta for your excellent advice on the 'Hope' chapter; Cassandra Pybus, Bob Gosford and Patricia Drescher for helping me to do the research for the history chapters; First Languages Australia for advice about Indigenous languages and for creating the Gambay Map; Bianca Valentino for her research and suggestions; Cathy Wilcox for her cartoon; and Simon Jackman for his analysis of the Voice referendum polling results. Thank you to designer Jenna Lee for another striking cover.

Sincere thanks to Djawa Yunupingu for sharing his brother Dr Yunupingu's words about Makarrata; and Noel Pearson for his powerful 2022 Boyer Lectures. Also Aaron Neal, Anastasia Urich, Merlin Chandra, Ngaree Blow, Eva Quilty, John Maynard, Terry O'Shane, Stacee Ketchell, Fiona Stanley, Jaki Adams, Charles Pakana Lara Watson, Uncle Steve Widders, the Monaghan family, Rebecca McCann, Jo Tarnawsky, Danny Gilbert, Rachel Perkins and Holly

Edwards for their general advice. To Mary Crooks and the Victorian Women's Trust, thank you for your tireless work. Thank you to Professor John Maynard and Armani Francois for writing the thoughtful forewords to this book.

And last but not least, I wish to express my great gratitude to the mentors and friends whose experience and wisdom has been most valuable, Marcia Langton, Kerry O'Brien and Peter Yu.

A note about the title

'Always was, Always will be Aboriginal land' is a slogan that I have shouted with thousands of Elders, brothers and sisters, and allies, at many a rally throughout my years of advocacy. I wanted a defiant title for this book. *Always Was, Always Will Be* is perfect. It is the plain truth.

In 2020, the words were used as the NAIDOC Week theme. Writing about the history of the theme for the Australian Museum, Laura McBride shared what is believed to be its genesis:

> The phrase originated during the 1980s Aboriginal land rights movement in far-western New South Wales. Barkandji people were fighting for legal recognition and rights as sovereign owners of their homelands. The late Uncle William Bates was a Barkandji land and legal rights activist. Along with other community members, Uncle William led the campaign that saw the first national park in NSW returned to Traditional Owners, amongst many other achievements for his people. In 1974 he became the first Aboriginal Legal Service field officer employed in Far West NSW (leading the breakaway along with Tombo Winters, Steve Gordon, and Uncle Alfie Bates in 1977, which resulted in the establishment of the Western Aboriginal

Legal Services) and rallied together communities and land councils to pool funds and start buying back their traditional lands. 'Always Was, Always Will Be', the now ubiquitous catchcry, was born during this time.

On one of the many trips out on Country during this land rights campaign, Uncle William's father, Uncle Jim Bates, became excited and started telling stories of his Country and land. Uncle William said, 'Dad, it's not your land anymore, whitefellas own it,' and Uncle Jim replied, 'No, they only borrowed it; it always was, and always will be Aboriginal land.'

–Director, First Nations, Australian Museum, Laura McBride,
a proud Wailwan and Kooma woman

About the author

Thomas Mayo is an Aboriginal and Torres Strait Islander man born on Larrakia country in Darwin. He is the elected Assistant National Secretary of the MUA, an award-winning author, essayist, orator and a signatory to the Uluṟu Statement from the Heart.

His advocacy and leadership in the push for the rights and recognition of Indigenous peoples span over twenty years.

Thomas has campaigned for the Uluṟu Statement's proposals of Voice, Treaty and Truth-Telling since it was created in May 2017. He was entrusted with taking the original Uluṟu Statement canvas around the country. Thomas was a leading spokesperson in the Yes campaign for the 2023 Voice referendum.

In addition to his trade union work and writing, Thomas is serving on the board of the Indigenous Literacy Foundation and Australians for Indigenous Constitutional Recognition.

The Voice to Parliament Handbook, written with Kerry O'Brien and with cartoons by Cathy Wilcox, was awarded Book of the Year, General Non-Fiction Book of the Year and Social Impact Book of the Year at the 2024 Australian Book Industry Awards (ABIA).